# First World War
### and Army of Occupation
# War Diary
### France, Belgium and Germany

21 DIVISION
110 Infantry Brigade
Duke of Edinburgh's (Wiltshire Regiment)
1st Battalion
1 July 1918 - 29 May 1919

WO95/2165/3

The Naval & Military Press Ltd
www.nmarchive.com
**Published in association with The National Archives**

Published by

## The Naval & Military Press Ltd

Unit 10 Ridgewood Industrial Park,

Uckfield, East Sussex,

TN22 5QE England

Tel: +44 (0) 1825 749494

www.naval-military-press.com

www.nmarchive.com

*This diary has been reprinted in facsimile from the original. Any imperfections are inevitably reproduced and the quality may fall short of modern type and cartographic standards.*

© **Crown Copyright**
**Images reproduced by permission of The National Archives, London, England, 2015.**

# Contents

| Document type | Place/Title | Date From | Date To |
|---|---|---|---|
| Heading | WO95/2165/3 | | |
| Heading | 21st Division 110th Infy Bde 1st Bn Wiltshire Regt Jly 1918-May 1919 From 25 Div 7 Bde | | |
| War Diary | Mille-Bosc | 01/07/1918 | 01/07/1918 |
| War Diary | Raincheval | 02/07/1918 | 16/07/1918 |
| War Diary | Acheux Wood | 17/07/1918 | 17/07/1918 |
| War Diary | Raincheval | 18/07/1918 | 19/07/1918 |
| War Diary | Forceville | 20/07/1918 | 20/07/1918 |
| War Diary | E. Of Acheux Wood | 22/07/1918 | 24/07/1918 |
| War Diary | Support Trenches N.E. Englebelmer | 25/07/1918 | 28/07/1918 |
| War Diary | N.E. Englebelmer | 29/07/1918 | 31/07/1918 |
| War Diary | Englebelmer Trench System | 01/08/1918 | 06/08/1918 |
| War Diary | Englebelmer | 11/08/1918 | 11/08/1918 |
| War Diary | Englebelmer Trench System | 12/08/1918 | 20/08/1918 |
| War Diary | Englebelmer | 21/08/1918 | 21/08/1918 |
| War Diary | Beaumont-Hamel | 22/08/1918 | 24/08/1918 |
| War Diary | Battery Valley | 24/08/1918 | 24/08/1918 |
| War Diary | Mirumont Ridge | 24/08/1918 | 24/08/1918 |
| War Diary | Destremont Farm | 25/08/1918 | 28/08/1918 |
| War Diary | Warlencourt | 29/08/1918 | 29/08/1918 |
| War Diary | West of Beaulencourt | 30/08/1918 | 31/08/1918 |
| Heading | War Diary September 1918 1st Bn Wiltshire Regt. Volume III Pages 5-9 | | |
| War Diary | Near Beaulencourt | 01/09/1918 | 01/09/1918 |
| War Diary | Beaulencourt | 03/09/1918 | 05/09/1918 |
| War Diary | Near Sailly-Saissisel | 07/09/1918 | 07/09/1918 |
| War Diary | Etricourt | 09/09/1918 | 09/09/1918 |
| War Diary | Near Sorel-Le-Grand. | 10/09/1918 | 10/09/1918 |
| War Diary | Heaudicourt | 11/09/1918 | 11/09/1918 |
| War Diary | Near Heudicourt | 13/09/1918 | 16/09/1918 |
| War Diary | Equan Court | 17/09/1918 | 18/09/1918 |
| War Diary | Near Heudicourt | 19/09/1918 | 19/09/1918 |
| War Diary | Near Etricourt | 24/09/1918 | 24/09/1918 |
| War Diary | Near-Sorel Le-Grand | 25/09/1918 | 25/09/1918 |
| War Diary | West of Gouzeaucourt | 28/09/1918 | 30/09/1918 |
| Miscellaneous | Attack on Beaulencourt On Sept 1st 1918. | 01/09/1918 | 01/09/1918 |
| Miscellaneous | Reference Sheet 57 C S E 1/20,000. | 30/09/1918 | 30/09/1918 |
| Heading | War Diary 1st Batt The Wiltshire Regt October 1918 Volume 3 Pages 10-13. | | |
| War Diary | Near Villers-Guislain | 01/10/1918 | 05/10/1918 |
| War Diary | Hindenburg Line. | 07/10/1918 | 08/10/1918 |
| War Diary | East Of Batouzelle | 08/10/1918 | 08/10/1918 |
| War Diary | Near Hurtebise Farm. | 09/10/1918 | 09/10/1918 |
| War Diary | Hurtebise Farm | 10/10/1918 | 10/10/1918 |
| War Diary | Caullery. | 11/10/1918 | 22/10/1918 |
| War Diary | Neuvilly. | 22/10/1918 | 22/10/1918 |
| War Diary | Nr. Ovillers | 23/10/1918 | 24/10/1918 |
| War Diary | Vendegies. | 25/10/1918 | 25/10/1918 |
| War Diary | Near Pois-Du-Nord. | 26/10/1918 | 26/10/1918 |
| War Diary | Ovillers | 27/10/1918 | 29/10/1918 |

| | | | |
|---|---|---|---|
| War Diary | Poix-Du-Nord. | 31/10/1918 | 31/10/1918 |
| Miscellaneous | Appendix. No.I. Operations 7th to 8th Oct. Sheet 57b S.W. 1/20000. | 07/10/1918 | 07/10/1918 |
| Miscellaneous | Appendix. No.2.Operations 22/23rd Oct. 1918. | 22/10/1918 | 22/10/1918 |
| Miscellaneous | 1st Battalion Wiltshire Regiment Awards during the month of October, 1918. | | |
| Miscellaneous | List of Officers at duty with Battalion during the month of October, 1918. | | |
| Heading | War Diary 1st Bn. The Wiltshire Regiment November, 1918. Volume 3. Pages 14-15 Vol 52 | | |
| War Diary | Poix-Du-Nord Amerval | 01/11/1918 | 04/11/1918 |
| War Diary | Nr. Engle-Fontaine La Tete Noir | 05/11/1918 | 06/11/1918 |
| War Diary | Nr. Aulnoye | 07/11/1918 | 07/11/1918 |
| War Diary | Aulnoye | 08/11/1918 | 08/11/1918 |
| War Diary | Berlaimont | 09/11/1918 | 11/11/1918 |
| War Diary | Beaufort | 12/11/1918 | 30/11/1918 |
| Operation(al) Order(s) | 1st Bn. The Wiltshire Regiment Operation Order No. 11. Appendix No. I | 02/11/1918 | 02/11/1918 |
| Operation(al) Order(s) | 1st Bn. Wiltshire Regiment Operation Order No 12 Appendix No 2 | 03/11/1918 | 03/11/1918 |
| Miscellaneous | Report On operations Nov. 4th to Nov. 7th. 1918 Appendix No 3 | 04/11/1918 | 04/11/1918 |
| Operation(al) Order(s) | 1st Bn. Wiltshire Regiment Operation Order No. 13. Appendix No. 4. | 07/11/1918 | 07/11/1918 |
| Operation(al) Order(s) | 1st Bn. Wiltshire Regiment Operation Order No. 14. Appendix No 5. | 10/11/1918 | 10/11/1918 |
| Miscellaneous | Special Order of The Day By General Hon. Sir J.H.G. Byng. K.C.B., K.C.M.G., M.V.O., Commanding Third Army. Appendix No. 6 | 11/11/1918 | 11/11/1918 |
| Miscellaneous | 110 Bde. G. 26/166 Appendix No 7 | 11/11/1918 | 11/11/1918 |
| Miscellaneous | 21st Division Special Order. Appendix No 8 | 11/11/1918 | 11/11/1918 |
| Miscellaneous | 110th Infantry Brigade Special Order of The Day. Appendix No 9 | 12/11/1918 | 12/11/1918 |
| Miscellaneous | 110th Bde. Q. 227/84. Appendix No 10 | 12/11/1918 | 12/11/1918 |
| Miscellaneous | 1st Battalion Wiltshire Regiment Awards during the month of November, 1918. | | |
| Miscellaneous | Noth | | |
| Miscellaneous | List of Officers at duty with the Battalion during the month of November | | |
| Heading | War Diary of 1st Bn Wiltshire Regiment. From:- 1st December 1918. To:- 31st December 1918. | | |
| War Diary | Beaufort | 01/12/1918 | 14/12/1918 |
| War Diary | Berliamont | 15/12/1918 | 15/12/1918 |
| War Diary | Vendigies | 16/12/1918 | 16/12/1918 |
| War Diary | Inchy | 17/12/1918 | 17/12/1918 |
| War Diary | Clairy | 17/12/1918 | 17/12/1918 |
| War Diary | Saulchoix | 21/12/1918 | 31/12/1918 |
| Miscellaneous | List of Officers at duty with the Battalion during the month of December | | |
| Miscellaneous | 1st Battalion Wiltshire Regiment Awards during the month of December, 1918 | | |
| Operation(al) Order(s) | 1st Bn Wiltshire Regt. Operation Order No. 15. Appendix No 1 | 12/12/1918 | 12/12/1918 |
| Operation(al) Order(s) | 1st Bn. Wiltshire Regiment. Operation Order No. 16. Appendix No 2 | | |
| Miscellaneous | 1st Bn. Wiltshire Regiment | | |

| Type | Description | Date From | Date To |
|---|---|---|---|
| Operation(al) Order(s) | 110th Inf. Bde. Order No. 180. Appendix No 1 | 10/12/1918 | 10/12/1918 |
| Miscellaneous | Table To Accompany 110th Inf. Bde. Order No. 180. | | |
| Operation(al) Order(s) | 110th Inf. Bde. Order No. 181. Appendix No 2 | 13/12/1918 | 13/12/1918 |
| Miscellaneous | Table "A" to accompany 110th Inf. Bde. Order No. 181. Appendix no. 2 | | |
| Miscellaneous | Table "B" to accompany 110th Inf. Bde. Order No. 181. Appendix No 3 | | |
| Operation(al) Order(s) | 110th Inf. Bde. Order No. 182. Appendix No 4 | 14/12/1918 | 14/12/1918 |
| Miscellaneous | Table accompanying 110th Inf. Bde. Order No. 182. Appendix No 4 | | |
| Miscellaneous | Appendix No 4 | | |
| Miscellaneous | Amended Table To Accompany 110th Inf. Bde. Order No. 182. Appendix No 4 | | |
| Operation(al) Order(s) | 1st Bn. Wiltshire Regiment Operations Order No. 17. Appendix No 4 | 16/12/1918 | 16/12/1918 |
| War Diary | Clairy Saulchoix | 01/01/1919 | 31/01/1919 |
| Heading | War Diary 1st Bn. Wiltshire Regiment February, 1919 Volume III Pages 19. | | |
| War Diary | Clairy-Saulchoix | 01/02/1919 | 28/02/1919 |
| Operation(al) Order(s) | Appendix No. 1 1st Bn. Wiltshire Regiment Operation Order No. 17. | 26/02/1919 | 26/02/1919 |
| Heading | War Diary 1st Bn. Wiltshire Regt. For The Month Of March, 1919. Volume III Page 20 | | |
| War Diary | Clairy-Saulchoix | 01/03/1919 | 31/03/1919 |
| Operation(al) Order(s) | 1st Bn Wiltshire Regiment Operation Order No. 18. | 07/03/1919 | 07/03/1919 |
| Heading | War Diary 1st Battalion Wiltshire Regiment For The Month Of April, 1919. Volume III Page 20. | | |
| War Diary | Bovelles | 01/04/1919 | 05/04/1919 |
| War Diary | Bouchon | 06/04/1919 | 30/04/1919 |
| Operation(al) Order(s) | 1st Bn. Wiltshire Regiment Operation Order No. 19. | 04/04/1919 | 04/04/1919 |
| Heading | War Diary 1st Battalion Wiltshire Regiment For The Month of May 1919. Volume III Page 22. | | |
| Miscellaneous | Officer i/c No:I Sub Section Record Office. H.Q. B.T. in F.&.F. | | |
| War Diary | Bouchon | 01/05/1919 | 24/05/1919 |
| War Diary | Harfluer | 25/05/1919 | 28/05/1919 |
| War Diary | Havre | 29/05/1919 | 29/05/1919 |
| Operation(al) Order(s) | 1st Battalion Wiltshire Regt. Operation Order No:20. | 23/05/1919 | 23/05/1919 |

W095/21653

21ST DIVISION
110TH INFY BDE

1ST BN. WILTSHIRE REGT

JLY 1918-MAY 1919

From 25 DIV 7 BDE

1ST. BN. WILTSHIRE REGT.

Army Form C. 2118.

110/8

WAR DIARY
or
INTELLIGENCE SUMMARY.
(Erase heading not required.)

1ST. BN. WILTSHIRE REGT.

July 1918

Instructions regarding War Diaries and Intelligence Summaries are contained in F. S. Regs., Part II. and the Staff Manual respectively. Title pages will be prepared in manuscript.

| Place | Date | Hour | Summary of Events and Information | Remarks and references to Appendices |
|---|---|---|---|---|
| | JULY | | | |
| MILLE-BOSC | 1 | | The Battalion left at 5.45 a.m. to proceed by train to 3rd. Army Area. The entrainment took place at 6.0 p.m. at EU station. | H.S.G |
| RAINCHEVAL | 2 | | The Regiment detrained at PUCHVILLERS at 2.0.a.m + marched to RAINCHEVAL where it was accommodated in huts in the village. | H.S.G |
| do. | 3 | | Training Commenced. The Division was in G.H.Q. Reserve but acting as left support division to the V Corps + was much ready to move at short notice to take up positions in the BROWN LINE. The Battalions sector was E.I.S.E. of BEAUSSART. | H.S.G |
| do. | 4 } 6 } | | Training Continued | H.S.G |
| do. | 7 | | Lt. Col. E. B. C. WARD, D.S.O. South Wales Borderers took over command of the Battalion. | H.S.G |
| do. | 8 } 15 } | | Training Continued. The Battalion suffered from an epidemic of influenza during this period. | H.S.G |
| do. | 16 | | The Battalion commenced to march to ACHEUX WOOD at 3.0pm. Owing to the intense heat, marching was extremely difficult + many men fell out. The move was completed by 5.15 p.m + the Battalion was accommodated in huts + bivouacs | H.S.G |

Army Form C. 2118.

# WAR DIARY
or
INTELLIGENCE SUMMARY.

(Erase heading not required.)

1ST. BN. WILTSHIRE REGT.

| Place | Date | Hour | Summary of Events and Information | Remarks and references to Appendices |
|---|---|---|---|---|
| ACHEUX WOOD. | JULY 17 | 6.0 a.m. | At 6.0 a.m. The Battalion commenced to move back to RAINCHEVAL. The march being complete by 8.0 a.m. The same billets were occupied as before. The remainder of the day was spent in resting. | H.C.C |
| RAINCHEVAL | 18. | | Training Pa. commenced. | |
| do. | 19. | 3.0 a.m | At 3.0 a.m the Battalion commenced to march to FORCEVILLE, the move being complete by 5.30 a.m. The companies were accommodated in dug-outs shelters in a trench 200" East of the village where H.Q. were billeted in house. At about 9.0 p.m. the village was shelled for about half-an-hour. Casualties 3 O.R. wounded. | H.C.C |
| FORCEVILLE | 20. | 8.30 a.m | At 8.30 a.m the Companies commenced to take up position in trenches shelters vacated by the 6th & 7th Leicestershire Regt., the move being completed by 12 noon. The Battalion was was accommodated in trenches about 500" East of ACHEUX WOOD. The vicinities of FORCEVILLE & W. of BEAUSSART were shelled at intervals during the day. At 8.30 p.m. Batt. H.Q. moved to a railway cutting 100" E. of ACHEUX WOOD, the move being complete by 10.0 p.m. Quiet night with strong rain storms. Casualties Officers 1 Wounded O.R. 1 died of wounds 3 wounded | H.C.C |

Army Form C. 2118.

# WAR DIARY
## of
## INTELLIGENCE SUMMARY.
(Erase heading not required.)

1ST. BN. WILTSHIRE REGT.

| Place | Date | Hour | Summary of Events and Information | Remarks and references to Appendices |
|---|---|---|---|---|
| E. of ACHEUX | 22 | | Training Re-Commenced. | KCC |
| WOOD | 23 | | Training Continued as far as weather conditions which were very bad, would allow. | KCC |
| do. | | | The establishment of Lewis Guns was increased from 24 to 36. | |
| do. | 24 | | The 21st Division commenced to relieve the 63rd R.N. Division in the line during the evening. The Battalion relieved the 4th Bedfordshire Regt. 100th Brigade, in support on the right sub. sector. The relief KCC was complete by 12 m.m. 'A' Coy was on the left, 'C' Coy in the centre, 'D' Coy on the right & 'B' Coy in reserve. | KCC |
| | | | Quiet night. | |
| Suffolk Trenches | 25 | | Quiet day. About 9.15 p.m. the enemy shelled the vicinities of Battalion Hd. & B Company with H.E. Casualties O.R. 1 wounded. | KCC |
| N.E. ENGLEBELMER | | | 9a.o. KCC | |
| do. | 26 | | Quiet day. Weather Bad. Casualties O.R. 1 wounded | KCC |
| do. | 27 | | Quiet day. Weather very wet. Casualties O.R. 2 wounded | |
| do. | 28 | | Quiet day. On the night of 28-29 the Battalion became distributed in depth, having taken over half of the 6th Leinsters front. The relief was complete at 2.15 a.m. on the 29. 'B' Coy was on the front line, 'A' Coy in support and 'D' Coy in reserve. No casualties. | 229 |

Army Form C. 2118.

# WAR DIARY
## or
## INTELLIGENCE SUMMARY

(Erase heading not required.)

**1ST. BN. WILTSHIRE REGT.**

| Place | Date | Hour | Summary of Events and Information | Remarks and references to Appendices |
|---|---|---|---|---|
| N.E. ENGLEBELMER | 29 | | Quiet day. Weather showery. About 9.30 h.m. on arrival of the ration lorry shelling with H.E. shrapnel and gas shells (mustard and phosgene) for two hours throughout the night. | A24 |
| do | 30 | | Quiet day. Weather fine. "A" Coy moved up in close support of "B" Coy. The Bn. sector was subject to light gas and H.E. shelling line invisibly Lt. (gassed slightly) | A24 |
| do | 31 | | Quiet day. Weather fine. About 5.30 a.m. "B" Coy was subject to a shower of about 22 H.E. shells, this was repeated at 9.30 a.m. and 4.15 a.m. Casualties 2 O.R. wounded. | A24 |

O.C. 1ST. BN. WILTSHIRE REGT.

# WAR DIARY or INTELLIGENCE SUMMARY.

Army Form C. 2118.

Volume III  Page 1

Instructions regarding War Diaries and Intelligence Summaries are contained in F.S. Regs., Part II. and the Staff Manual respectively. Title pages will be prepared in manuscript.

(Erase heading not required.)

| Place | Date | Hour | Summary of Events and Information | Remarks and references to Appendices |
|---|---|---|---|---|
| ENGLEBELMER TRENCH SYSTEM | 1 | | Strength - Officers 40  O.R. 908. | |
| do | 5 | | Batt relieved by 6th Batt The Hertfordshire Regt in the Left Sub-sector and proceeded to the Purple Line at ENGLEBELMER | |
| do | 6 | 2.40 | Relief complete at Batt HQ totalities at (Q.19.6.55) (map Sheet 57d S.E.) | |
| ENGLEBELMER | 11 | 22.15 | Batt relieved the 4th Batt The Worcestershire Regt in the Right Sub-section Batt HQ 2 dolaterets at Q.26.a.59 (map Sheet 57d S.E.) | |
| ENGLEBELMER TRENCH SYSTEM | 12 | 2.00 | Relief complete. | |
| do | 13 | | Major L.C. CANNON M.C. Queen's Regt left to join 59 Division Major J.N. MUIRHEAD C.90 1st Lancers assumed command during the absence of Lieut. Col. G.R. CONNOR D.S.O. THE WILTS REGT | |
| do | 14 | 10.00 | Information received that the enemy was withdrawing from his positions and that the situation was to be at once confirmed on the Brigade Front. 2 fighting patrols under 2/Lt ST DAVID and A/t STEWART at once pushed out into THIEPVAL VILLAGE R26a and the Cemetery at N30.c.6.2 (map Sheet 57d S.E.) as dispatches. Patrols was established at Q23.c.58 and Q.24.c.36 (map Sheet 57d S.E.) | |
| do | 15 | 12.00 | Patrols from the posts established on the 14th were landed forwards. The troillere patrol | |

P. Stewart

# WAR DIARY
## or
## INTELLIGENCE SUMMARY

Army Form C. 2118.

Volume III  Page 2

(Erase heading not required.)

| Place | Date | Hour | Summary of Events and Information | Remarks and references to Appendices |
|---|---|---|---|---|
| ENGLEBELMER | 15 | | Under 2/Lt SGNALL proceeded around broken edge of THIEPVAL WOOD and reached R.25.a.95 but was driven in | |
| TRENCH SYSTEM | | | Withdrew through THIEPVAL WOOD to railway embankment at Q.25.b.91. Southern Patrol under 2/Lt ST DOWSON | |
| | | | proceeded around Southern edge of THIEPVAL WOOD but was cut off by the enemy and the whole Patrol | |
| | | | captured. Casualties killed Officers - NIL OR 1. Wounded Officers NIL - OR 6. Missing Officers 2/Lt ST DOWSON - | JATWm |
| | | | OR 22. | JATWm |
| do | 20 | | Batt relieved in Right Subsection by the 14th Batt THE WELSH REGT | JATWm |
| ENGELBELMER | 21 | 2.30 | Relief complete | JATWm |
| do | | | Batt proceeded to Brigade reserve at ENGELBELMER Batt HQ established at Q.19.6.6.5 (map sheet 57°5.E) | JATWm |
| do | | 15.00 | Batt less Drawshop proceeded by march route to BEAUMONT-HAMEL to be in reserve to the 64 Inf | JATWm |
| | | | Bde. who were attacking MIRAUMONT Batt HQ established at Q.54.44 (map sheet 57°5.E) | JATWm |
| BEAUMONT-HAMEL | 22 | 21.00 | Batt took up a position in LUMINOUS AVENUE N12.a..6 ready to support a counter attack as | |
| | | | enemy was reported to have broken through our Brown Line. Situation was restored by the | |
| | | | 63 Inf Bde and Batt returned to BEAUMONT-HAMEL (map sheet 57°5.E) Casualties killed - NIL | JATWm |
| | | | Wounded Officers 2/Lt S.C.WALL OR 6 Missing NIL | |
| do | 24 | 1.00 | Batt proceeded via LUMINOUS AVENUE to cross the Rue AMCRE at R.7.c.8.5 and come into | JATWm |
| | | | BATTERY VALLEY R.5.d - R.11.6 and proceed to advance (map sheet 57°S.G) | JATWm |

# WAR DIARY
## or
## INTELLIGENCE SUMMARY.

Army Form C. 2118.

Volume III Page 3

*(Erase heading not required.)*

| Place | Date | Hour | Summary of Events and Information | Remarks and references to Appendices |
|---|---|---|---|---|
| BATTERY VALLEY | 24 | 8.00 | Batt advanced to R16a and R16a in support of 1st Batt who had taken the hill south of MIRAUMONT | Jstm |
|  |  |  | in R11 & R17 but who had been unable to hold it. (Map Sheet 57° S.E.) |  |
|  | 24 | 13.00 | Batt advanced and took up position on MIRAUMONT RIDGE in Q11c and R at M16 & R14 a (Sheet 57°S.E) |  |
|  |  |  | Front line was established in this position. CASUALTIES Killed Officers NIL OR 5. Wounded Officers | Jstm |
|  |  |  | 3/Lt PL HOWE OR 15. Missing NIL. |  |
| MIRAUMONT RIDGE | 24 | 22.00 | Batt advanced in Artillery formation across the open ground in M4 and M5 (Map Sheet 57°SW) |  |
|  |  |  | to get in touch with the enemy and took up a position on the West of LE SARS |  |
|  |  |  | Bn in M15c and M15d (Map Sheet 57° S.W) Batt HQ established at M20 a 54. Touch with the | Jstm |
|  |  |  | enemy gained at DESIRÉMONT FARM M21a (Map Sheet 57° S.W.) |  |
| DESIREMONT FARM | 25 | 16.00 | Batt formed up West of DESIREMONT FARM to repel counter attack on FAUCOURT L'ABBAYE M23 central (Map Sheet 57°SW) Jstm |  |
| do | 25 | 17.00 | Batt withdrawn to Brigade Reserve in M14c 82 and M14 & 82 Batt HQ established at M14 d 8.9 (Map Sheet 57°SW) | Jstm |
| do | 25 | 22.00 | Batt relieved 1st Batt THE LINCOLNSHIRE REGT in the front line. Batt HQ established at M17 & 62 |  |
|  |  |  | (Map Sheet 57°SW) Relief complete 23 30 | Jstm |
| WARLENCOURT | 29 | 12.00 | Batt advanced by Bounds in direction of BEAULENCOURT M17 (Sheet 57°SW) D Coy acting |  |
|  |  |  | advance guard supported by A and C Coys with B Coy in reserve. 1st Bound LUISENHOF |  |
|  |  |  | FARM RD N13d-N19b. 2nd Bound Sunken Road from N21a - N15c. 3rd Bound N12a 50 |  |

P. Stanl LT. COLONEL
Comdg. 1st Bn. WILTSHIRE REGT.

**WAR DIARY** or **INTELLIGENCE SUMMARY.** VOLUME III PAGE 4

Army Form C. 2118.

| Place | Date | Hour | Summary of Events and Information | Remarks and references to Appendices |
|---|---|---|---|---|
| | 29 | | TRENCH in N16c L" BOUND N24a 51. – along BEAULENCOURT ROAD to N15 A.10. No opposition was encountered until the 3rd Round had been reached when the Battalion came under very heavy machine gun fire from BEAULENCOURT and heavy shell fire. The Battalion consolidated on the 3rd Objective and maintained the front line here (Map Sheet 57c S.W.) CASUALTIES KILLED Officers NIL O.R. NIL WOUNDED Officers MAJOR J A MUIRHEAD D.S.O. LIEUT E NEALE 2/Lt P L HUNT 2/Lt E J DUDLEY (at DUTY) O.R. 14 MISSING Officers NIL O.R. NIL MAJOR G T PARKES M.C. assumed command of the Battalion. | Appx |
| West of BEAULENCOURT | 30 | | Fighting Patrols sent out from forward companies to get in touch with enemy. Now BEAULENCOURT. Enemy discovered to be holding BEAULENCOURT very strongly. CASUALTIES KILLED Officers 2/Lt D H DAVIES O.R. 1 WOUNDED Officers NIL O.R. 4 MISSING Officers NIL O.R. NIL | Appx |
| do | 31 | 21.00 | Battn relieved by 1st Batt EAST YORKS REGT Relief complete 23.45 | Appx |
| | | | On completion of relief Battn moved to take up assembly positions east from N46 55 – N4d 34 (Map Sheet 57c S.W.) for attack on BEAULENCOURT. | Appx |
| do | 31 | - | Strength Officers 39 O.R. 723. | Appx |

LT. COLONEL
1st Bn. WILTSHIRE REGT.

CONFIDENTIAL

110/21

# WAR DIARY

SEPTEMBER 1918

1ˢᵗ Bⁿ WILTSHIRE REGᵗ

VOLUME III
Pages 5-9

Army Form C. 2118.

# WAR DIARY
## or
## ~~INTELLIGENCE SUMMARY~~

VOLUME III Page 5

(Erase heading not required.)

Vol 50

Instructions regarding War Diaries and Intelligence Summaries are contained in F. S. Regs., Part II. and the Staff Manual respectively. Title pages will be prepared in manuscript.

| Place | Date | Hour | Summary of Events and Information | Remarks and references to Appendices |
|---|---|---|---|---|
| NEAR BEAULENCOURT | 1 | | STRENGTH – Officers 37 O/Ranks. 823. | J. Thu |
| | | 0200 | Battalion formed up on road from N4.c.55 to N4.d.3.7. (Map Sheet 57c S.W) | J. Thu |
| | | | Battalion attached BEAULENCOURT and captured village. | J. Thu Appendix H°1. |
| | | | Casualties: Killed – Officers 2Lt. A.W. HENLEY – Other ranks 17. Wounded Officers – | |
| | | | 2Lt. J.G. PITT O/Ranks 41 – Missing Officers Nil O/Ranks 1. | |
| | | | Captured War material. 2 Field Guns 2 Light Field Guns 2 Heavy machine | |
| | | | Guns 20 Light machine Guns 5 Anti Tank Guns | |
| | | | Prisoners taken Officers 3 Other ranks 100 (approx) | |
| | | 1500. | Battalion H.Q. established in Quarry at N16.d.8.2 (Map Sheet 57c) | J. Thu |
| BEAULENCOURT | 3 | 2100. | Defences of BEAULENCOURT taken over by 6th Bn LEICESTERSHIRE REGT. | J. Thu |
| | | | Battalion withdrew to trenches at N.15 d – N.16 central (Map sheet 57c) | |
| | | | Bn. H.Q established at N.16.a.30 (Map Sheet 57c) | |
| BEAULENCOURT | 4 | 700 | Bn moved to Hutment Camp at N.11.C.9.6. (Map sheet 57c) | J. Thu |
| do. | 5 | 17.30 | Bn proceeded by march route to out skirts of SAILLY – SAISSISEL | J. Thu |
| | | | U.14.a (Sheet 57c) and bivouacked in trenches from U.11.d – U.11.9 | |
| | | | Bn HQ established at U.2.c.15.14 (Map Sheet 57c) | |

T.L. COLONEL,
COMDG 1st Bn. WILTSHIRE REGT

Army Form C. 2118.

# WAR DIARY
## OF
## INTELLIGENCE SUMMARY.

(Erase heading not required.)

VOLUME III  PAGE 6

| Place | Date | Hour | Summary of Events and Information | Remarks and references to Appendices |
|---|---|---|---|---|
| NEAR SAILLY-SAISSISEL. | 7 | 17.15 | Battalion proceeded by march route to ETRICOURT V 8 a (Sheet Map 57c) Bn H.Q. established at V 7 & 7.3 (Sheet 57c) | |
| ETRICOURT | 9 | 04.30 | Bn proceeded by march route to SOREL-LE-GRAND V 13 o (Map Sheet 57c) and bivouaced in valley in V 24 (Sheet 57c) Bn HQ established at V 25 c & 7 Sheet 67c. Bn under tactical command of 6th Infy Bde. | |
| Near SOREL-LE-GRAND. | 10 | 20.30 | Battalion relieved 15th Bn Durham Light Infantry Regt and 2nd Bn Kings Own Yorkshire Light Infantry Regt in front line system. | |
| HEUDICOURT | 11 | 03.00 | Relief complete. Bn HQ established at W 9 d. 99 (map Sheet 57c) | |
| Near HEUDICOURT | 13 | 10.00 | Enemy opened a heavy barrage on and behind our line and attacked under cover of flame projectors. The attack consisted of two strong parties, the northern party worked down reserve trench and attacked 'D' Company at the junction between D' Company and Division on our left. The southern party worked along CAVALRY SUPPORT and attacked 'C' Company at the junction between 'C' Company and attached 'C' Company at the junction left post of 'D' Company and Battalion on our right. The two Companies were forced to withdraw, but a | |

Army Form C. 2118.

# WAR DIARY
## or
## INTELLIGENCE SUMMARY.    VOLUME III   Page I

(Erase heading not required.)

| Place | Date | Hour | Summary of Events and Information | Remarks and references to Appendices |
|---|---|---|---|---|
| Near HEUDECOURT | 13 | 10.00 | A counter attack was at once organized and original line restored. The Southern party was driven off without difficulty. Casualties:- KILLED Officers NIL. O/Rs 3. WOUNDED Officers Biewt R.H. HAMLETT, 2Lieut A.E. THOMPSON (at duty) O/Rs 22. MISSING Officers NIL O/Rs 1. Captures:- Personnel Prisoners 10. War material 1 Machine Gun | |
| -do- | 15 | 21.00 | Bn relieved by 5th Bn Scottish Rifles. Casualties KILLED NIL. Wounded Officer 2Lieut W.H. POSTGATE O/Rs 4 MISSING NIL. | 347m |
| -do- | 16 | 04.30 | Relief complete. Bn proceeded to Camp at V.16.a.7.c. Bn H.Q. established at V.16.a.8.1 (Map Sheet 57c S.E.) Camp heavily shelled. Bn moved to V.9.c. (Sheet 57c) | 347m |
| EPRANCOURT | 17 | 20.00 | Bn proceeded by march route to take up assembly positions in W.23.6 in preparation for an attack | 347m |
| -do- | 18 | 04.30 | Move to assembly positions completed. Bn H.Q. established at W.23.6.1.0 (Sheet 57c) | 347m |
| Near HERUNCOURT | 18 | 05.20 | Bn attacked in conjunction with other Bns under cover of our barrage. Casualties - KILLED Officers NIL - O/Rs 13 WOUNDED - | 347m |

Lt. COLONEL,
COMDG. 1st Bn. WILTSHIRE REGT.

# WAR DIARY
## or
## INTELLIGENCE SUMMARY.

*(Erase heading not required.)*

Army Form C. 2118.

VOLUME III   Page 8

| Place | Date | Hour | Summary of Events and Information | Remarks and references to Appendices |
|---|---|---|---|---|
| NEAR HEUDICOURT | 18 | | Officers - Capt. B.C. MACKIE, Lieut. D.F. BROWN, 2/Lieut. J. CARNEY, 2/Lieut. J.C. KEMP O/R's 71 MISSING Officers NIL O/R's 8. Captures Personnel 4 Officers 220 O/R's War Material 8 Field Guns | Appendix No 2. |
| | 19 | 22.00 | Bn relieved by 1st Bn CAMERONIAN REGT. | 35th |
| | | 23.00 | Relief complete. Bn proceeded by march route to D.6.d (Map Sheet 57c) | 35th |
| NEAR ETRICOURT | 24 | 16.00 | Bn proceeded by march route to Hutment Camp at V.29.a (Sheet 57c) | 35th |
| NEAR-SOREL LE-GRAND | 25 | 19.30 | Bn moved forward to take up a position in HEATHER and LOWLAND Trenches from W.5.d.05.95 — W.12.a.0.0. Bn H.Q. established at W.10.b.0.8. (Sheet 57c S.E.) | 35th |
| WEST OF GOUZEAUCOURT | 28 | 02.00 | Bn proceeded by march route to assembly places at X.26.7.d for attack on Green Line from X.5.c.35.50 to R.31.d.9.9 but owing to leading Battalion failing to take its objective the Bn was unable to reach its assembly position and carry out attack. The Bn withdrew to Sunken road. | 35th |

Lt. COLONEL
COMDG. 1st Bn. WILTSHIRE Rgt.

# WAR DIARY
## or
## INTELLIGENCE SUMMARY.

Army Form C. 2118.

VOLUME III Page 9

| Place | Date | Hour | Summary of Events and Information | Remarks and references to Appendices |
|---|---|---|---|---|
| WEST OF GONZEAUCOURT | 28 | | in W.6.b. (Sheet 57c S.E.) | |
| do. | | 10.00 | Battalion came under tactical command of 62nd Inf Bde and proceeded to R.25 Central with orders to proceed from thus to assembly position in Sunken road at R.27 a & b in order to attack enemy trenches in R.28 thus cutting off enemy retreat from GONNELIEU. On arriving in the neighbourhood of R.25 Central it was discovered that the enemy was still holding trench system in R.27 a & b so that the attack was impossible. Bn took up a position in FERN BLOCK R.21 c. Bn H.Q. established at R.20.a.8.6. (Map Sheet 57c SE) | JHW |
| | 28. | 20.00 | Bn. returned to sunken road W.6.2.d (Sheet 57c S.E.) | JHW |
| | 30. | | STRENGTH Officers 34 O/Rs.731 | |

J.H.W.
Lt. COLONEL,
COMDG. 1st Bn. WILTSHIRE REGT.

Appendix No 1

## Attack on BEAULENCOURT on Sept 1st 1918.

The Battn marched to its forming up position and formed up on the road from N.4.c.5.5. to N.4.d.3.7. in the following order:-

   Front Line   B Coy (under Capt. C.H. Gaskell) on the right
                    A Coy (under Capt. H.B. Brown) on the left.
   Support Line  C Coy (under 2/Lt. F.G. Pitt) on the left
                    D Coy (under Capt. E.J. Brewer) on the right.

At 2.00 am a creeping barrage was put down on a line N.11.d.0.0. to N.12.a.0.0. and remained there for 20 minutes. At the same time heavy Artillery bombarded BEAULENCOURT and the high ground to the East of it.

The Battn went forward under the barrage in extended order and attacked the village.

Battn H.Q. were established in the trench at N.11.d.9.0.

The village was strongly held by enemy Machine Guns but the Battn attacked with such determination that the opposition was overcome and by 5.30 am the village was in our hands.

A Coy at once consolidated in the trench from N.18.c.2.7. to N.17.d.9.4 and D Coy came up on its right and held a series of Platoon Posts from N.17.d.9.4 to N.17.d.0.5 and C Coy after mopping up the village took up a position in reserve in the Sunken road in N.17.c. B Coy pushed forward on the left flank and held a very advanced position in N.18.c until on 1/2 Sept. when they withdrew to re-organise in the village. Our right flank was protected by a section of M.Gs from A Coy 21st M.G. Battn., who took up a position from N.17.d.5.3 to N.17.c.5.2.

At 6.30 the enemy attempted a counter-attack under cover of a smoke barrage, but it was easily repulsed.

The following war material was captured in the village.

| | |
|---|---|
| 2 Field Guns (Damaged) | 21 Light Machine Guns. |
| 2 Light Field Pieces | 5 Anti-Tank Rifles. |
| 2 Heavy Machine Guns. | |

Page 2.

Approx: 100 Prisoners were captured including 4 Officers.

Our casualties were:-

    Killed: Officers  2/Lt. A.W. Healey.
              ORs      17.
    Wounded Officers  2/Lt. F.G. Pitt.
               ORs     41.
    Missing Officers  Nil
               ORs     1.

After the village of BEAULENCOURT had been captured the enemy resistance entirely broke down and the neighbouring villages of LE TRANSLOY and VILLERS-AU-FLOS were soon taken and the Divisions on either flanks swept forward after the enemy.

                                              Lt. Colonel.
                              Comdg 1st Bn Wiltshire Regt.

Reference Sheet 57 C SE
1/20,000.

At 8pm on the 17th the Battalion marched from its Bivouac at Valley Copse (V.9.a.2.0.) to the FINS–NURLU road (V.17.d.4.1.) and at that spot picked up a Taped Track leading south of SOREL-le-GRAND and HEUDECOURT to a point on the railway W.23.a.5.2. At the commencement the track was clearly laid, the night fine and the marching was good. At 10.20 pm the Brigade sent orders for the Battalion to halt and clear the track so as to allow a Battalion of the 62nd Inf Bde to pass through. This Battalion passed through at 1.50 am 18th. It had commenced to rain, the track was laid across the sunken road, the men had great difficulty in crossing and there was considerable delay. At about 400 yards from the railway the tape ended, the track being marked by posts only and they at wide intervals; it had become very dark and the companies kept on missing the track.

The Battalion formed up facing east on a line 300yds east of trenches in W.24.a. The 6th Bn Leicestershire Regt was to the south of the Railway and on the same alignment. The 62nd Infantry Brigade was drawn up in front. At 5.20 am the Barrage opened, the 62nd Inf Bde attacked the Trenches on the western and eastern slopes of the High Ground in X.13.c. X.19.a and c. The Battalion and 6th Leicesters followed them closely until they reached the sunken road and railway cutting in W.24.b. and X.19.a. When the 62nd Inf Bde completed the capture of their objective, the Battalion advanced covered by a creeping Barrage the objective being LIMERICK TRENCH X.21.b.4.2. to LEITH WALK X.15.d.5.9. On our right the 6th Leicestershire Regt on the left 64th Infantry Brigade. The 7th Bn Leicestershire Regt were in Brigade Reserve.

The Capture of the objective was to be carried out as follows. A. and C. Coys under cover of the Barrage capture MEATH POST. With bombing parties and artillery support the Companies were to work outwards and establish touch with troops on our flanks. B. Coy mop up LINNET VALLEY and reinforce the front line D Company in support.

The following actually took place A. and C. captured MEATH POST and worked outwards according to plan. The troops on our flanks had not come up – our bombing parties were driven back and MEATH POST was counterattacked in strength. A & C withdrew and took up a position in MEATH LANE and the ridge in X.15.a. X.20.b. X.21.a.

B. Coy cleared LINNET VALLEY and reinforced the front line, D Coy in support in road X.20.b & d: with Bn HQ in same place.

J.W.Reed Lt Col
O.C. 1st Bn Wiltshire Regt

30/9/18

Confidential

# War Diary
## 1st Batt The Wiltshire Regt
### October 1918

Volume 3

Pages 10-13

# WAR DIARY

## INTELLIGENCE SUMMARY

*(Erase heading not required.)*

Army Form C. 2118.

1st Bn. Wiltshire Regiment.

Volume 3. Page 10.

| Place | Date | Hour | Summary of Events and Information | Remarks and references to Appendices |
|---|---|---|---|---|
| Near VILLERS-GUISLAIN | 1st. | | Strength. Officers-34. Other ranks-727. Horses-49, Mules-3. | |
| | 2nd. | 18.30 | Battalion relieved 7th Bn. LEICESTERSHIRE REGT in front line system from X.5.c.4.3. to R.34.b.9.0.(Map sheet 57c S.E.) Battn Headquarters established in KITCHEN CRATER R.33.c.8.5. (Map sheet 57c S.E.) Draft of 5 Officers and 151 other ranks arrived at Divisional Reception Camp. | |
| | 5th. | 09.30 | Patrols pushed across the Canal De L'escaut at M.3Id and discovered that the enemy had evacuated the East Banks of Canal. | |
| | | 12.00 | Battalion moved forward and occupied HINDENBURG LINE. Battn H.Q. established at M.32b50 (sheet 57b Strength- Officers-34. Other ranks 855. Horses 48, Mules 3. | |
| HINDENBURG LINE. | 7th | 22.00 | Battalion moved forward to forming up position East of MONTECOUVER FARM (N 3Ic(sheet 57b) for attack on enemy position in the BEAUREVOIR LINE. | |
| | 8th. | 1.00 | Battalion attacked BEAUREVOIR LINE after heavy bombardment by our Artillery. Battalion met with resistance from enemy Machine Gun Posts but succeeded in reaching and maintaining all its objectives. | Appendix No 1. |
| | | 6.00. | 6th and 7th Battns THE LEICESTERSHIRE REGT formed up behind the line which we had taken and attacked the BEAUREVOIR LINE as far as HURTEBISE FARM (N.14d. sheet 57b) | |
| | | 8.00 | 62nd INF.BDE. passed through line held by 110th INF. BDE. and pushed forward and established a line east of WALINGCOURT (N.24. sheet 57b). | |
| | | | CASUALTIES. Killed. Officers 2/Lt. R. Hall. Other ranks 11. Wounded. Officers 2/Lt. J.T.Luscombe (At duty) Capt. W.C.Rowe, 2/Lt F.G.Comfort. Wounded. Other ranks. 78. Missing Officers. NIL. Other ranks. 2. | |
| | | | CAPTURES. - PERSONNEL.- NIL. Other ranks. 81. MATERIAL.- T.M.B.-I. Machine Guns.-2. | |

Lt.COLONEL,
COMDG. 1st Bn. WILTSHIRE REGT.

Army Form C.2118.

# WAR DIARY
## or
## INTELLIGENCE SUMMARY

1st Bn. Wiltshire Regiment.

Volume 3. Page II.

(Erase heading not required.)

Instructions regarding War Diaries and Intelligence Summaries are contained in F.S. Regs., Part II. and the Staff Manual respectively. Title Pages will be prepared in manuscript.

| Place | Date | Hour | Summary of Events and Information | Remarks and references to Appendices |
|---|---|---|---|---|
| EAST OF BATOUZELLE | 8th | 15.00 | Orders received for Battn. to concentrate in N.14c (sheet 57c) in order to advance for attack High Ground in N.18c | Jshm. |
| | | 16.00 | Battn concentrated as ordered. | Jshm. |
| | | 17.00 | Attack orders cancelled. Battn ordered to support 1st BN. LINCOLNSHIRE REGT who were carrying out attack on WALINCOURT. | Jshm. |
| | | 19.00 | Three Coys took up position in HURTEBISE COPSE (N.21b sheet 57b) One Coy went forward to S.E. corner of BRISEUX WOOD to support attack on GUILLEMIN FARM. Battn H.Q. established at N.21.3.5. | Jshm. |
| NEAR HURTEBISE FARM. | 9th | 03.00 | The 17th Division passed through the 21st Division | Jshm. |
| | | 09.00 | Battalion ordered to concentrate in N.21. Battalion H.Q. established in HURTEBISE FARM N.14.0 (sheet 57b). | Jshm. |
| HURTEBISE FARM | 10th | 15.00 | Battalion moved forward by march route to CAULLERY. Battalion H.Q. established at 12 Rue-de-SAC O 13.a.5.0.(sheet 57c). | Jshm. |
| CAULLERY. | 11th 12th 13th | | Strength Officers.32, other ranks 767, horses 49v, mules 3. Reorganisation and training commenced. Lt/Col G.B.C. Ward D.S.O. assumed command of 110th INF.BDE during the absence of Brig-Gen H. Cummings D.S.O. Major T.G. Parkes M.C. assumed command of the Battalion. | Jshm. Jshm. Jshm. |
| | 19th | | Strength. Officers-32 other ranks 755, Horses 49, mules 3. | Jshm. |
| | 22nd | 09.00 | Battalion proceeded by march route to take up assembly position for attack on OVILLERS and RED LINE W. of VENDIGIES-AU-BOIS. Battalion halted at mid-day at INCHY (map ref. J22 central, sheet 57b N.E.) where B. Echelon of transport remained. Battalion with Echelon A. proceeded to NEUVILLY (map ref. K.8. sheet 57b N.E.) where a halt was made for tea. | Jshm. |
| NEUVILLY. | 22nd | 22.00 | Battalion proceeded to assembly position in sunken road E.28c. | Jshm. |
| NR. OVVILLERS | 23 | 03.00 | Battalion in conjunction with 7th Battn LEICESTERSHIRE REGT on the left and 64th INF. BDE on the right attacked red dotted line W. of OVILLERS and red line W.of VENDIGIES-AU-BOIS. Battalion succeeded in taking all its objectives and held them until 6th BATTN The LEICESTERSHIRE REGT and 62nd INF. BDE went through to capture further objectives | APPENDIX Nº2. Jshm. |

J. Martin Day, Lt. COLONEL,
COMDG. 1st Bn. WILTSHIRE REGT.

2449 Wt. W14957/M90 750,000 1/16 J.B.C. & A. Forms/C.2118/12.

Army Form C. 2118.

1st Bn. Wiltshire Regiment.

Volume 3.  Page. 12

# WAR DIARY
## or
## INTELLIGENCE SUMMARY

*(Erase heading not required.)*

Instructions regarding War Diaries and Intelligence Summaries are contained in F. S. Regs., Part II. and the Staff Manual respectively. Title Pages will be prepared in manuscript.

| Place | Date | Hour | Summary of Events and Information | Remarks and references to Appendices |
|---|---|---|---|---|
| NR. OVILLERS Ctd | 23rd | 02.00 | Casualties. Killed-Officers. 2/Lt. H.R.Palmer, 2/Lt. H. B. Cooper. Other ranks-23. Wounded. do - Lt.W.J.E.Ross. 2/Lt E.G. Blackmore, 2/Lt H.Aston.- Other ranks.I20. Missing. do - NIL. Other ranks, - 7. | |
| NR. OVILLERS. | | 16.00 | Battalion took over defence of RED LINE. Batt. H.Q. established at E.23.c.8.2. (Map sheet 57b.N.E.) | |
| | 24th | 01.00 | Battalion proceeded by march route to POIX-DU-NORD to take up position in preparation to act as Advance Guard for IIO INF.BDE when objectives of 64th INF. BDE had been captured. The 64th INF. BDE were unable to take their objectives and the Battalion withdrew to occupy the Green Line W. of POIS-DU-NORD. Battalion H.Q. established at VENDEGIES F.7d 2.9. (sheet 57b N.E.) | |
| | | | Casualties. Killed- Officers.- NIL.   Other ranks. NIL. Wounded- do - Lieut. G. Cartwright.   Other ranks. 9. Missing- do - NIL          do   do   NIL | |
| VENDEGIES. | 25th | 07.00 | C. Coy went forward to BROWN LINE (ARBRE-DE-LA-CROIX - LESTUILERIES) x 28b - X29c (sheet 5Ia S.E.) with orders to be prepared to push forward patrols if enemy retired. | |
| | | 16.00 | Battalion relieved the 12/13 BTNS THE NORTHUMBERLAND FUSILIERS on the left of the Divisional front, from halt at XII central to Fork Road at XI7b. (sheet 5Ia. S.E. Relief complete at 22.00 hours. Battalion H.Q. established at X21 d. 9.7. | |
| NEAR POIS-DU-NORD. | 26th. | 18.00 | Battalion relieved by I0th Battalion LANCASHIRE FUSILERS on the left of the Divisional Front. Relief complete at 21.30 hours. Battalion proceeded on relief to billets at OVILLERS. Battalion H.Q. established at F. 24.8. I9. | |
| | | | Casualties. Killed- Officers.- NIL.   Other ranks. NIL. Wounded- do - NIL.   Other ranks. 2. Missing. do - NIL.   Other ranks. NIL | |
| OVILLERS | 27th 28th 29th. | | Reorganisation and training commenced. Major. T.G. Parkes.M.C. assumed command of the Battalion during the absence of Lt/Col G.B.C.Ward D.S.O. on leave. | |
| | 29th. | I5.30 | Battalion less Transport proceeded by march route to be in Bde reserve in POIX-DU-NORD. | |

COMD 1st Bn WILTSHIRE REGT.

Army Form C. 2118.

# WAR DIARY
## or
## INTELLIGENCE SUMMARY

1st Bn. Wiltshire Regiment.

Volume 3. Page 13.

*(Erase heading not required.)*

Instructions regarding War Diaries and Intelligence Summaries are contained in F. S. Regs., Part II and the Staff Manual respectively. Title Pages will be prepared in manuscript.

| Place | Date | Hour | Summary of Events and Information | Remarks and references to Appendices |
|---|---|---|---|---|
| OVILLERS Contd. | 29th | 15.30 | Battalion H.Q. established at F.4.a 2.5. (map sheet 57b. N.E. | |
| | | 23.00 | Enemy bombarded POIX-DU-NORD with heavy Artillery. | |
| | | | Casualties. Killed.- Officers. NIL. Other ranks 2. | |
| | | | Wounded.- Officers. NIL. Other ranks. K. 8. | |
| | | | Missing.- Officers. NIL. Other ranks. NIL | |
| POIX-DU-NORD. | 31st | 15.30. | Enemy again bombarded POIX-DU-NORD with heavy Artillery. | |
| | | | Casualties. Killed.- Officers. NIL. Other ranks. 1. | |
| | | | Wounded.- Officers. NIL. Other ranks. 13. | |
| | | | Missing.- Officers. NIL. Other ranks. NIL. | |
| | | | Strength.- Officers 29 Other ranks. 559. Horses 48. Mules. 3 | |

J. Charles Major
Lt. COLONEL,
COMDG. 1st Bn. WILTSHIRE REGT.

## APPENDIX. NO. I.

### OPERATIONS 7th to 8th OCT.
### Sheet 57b S.W. 1/20000.

The Battalion was situated in the HINDENBURG SUPPORT LINE from RANCOURT FARM exclusive to the light railway in M.33.d. Battalion H.Q. established at M.32b.4.I. . The 7th BTN THE LEICESTERSHIRE REGT was on the left, the 33rd DIV. on the right, and the 6th BTN LEICESTERSHIRE REGT in support at M33.c.

The 64th INF.BDE, was holding the front line MOUNTECOUVEZ FARM inclusive through N25 central.

The objective for the Battalion was a line from N.33.c.2.8 to N.33.a.2I.7. and from there a defensive flank to N.32.0.8.

The Companies were to rendezvous on the eastern edge of the RANCOURT COPSE at 22.45 hours. Owing to the very dark night and the amount of wire to be passed through the rendezvous was not completed til 23.30 hours. The Companies then moved off in column of route with increased distances via the tracks and roads M.35c.-M.35b-M.36.a.c.d. and to the sunken road N.3Ia.

Owing to the darkness state of roads and other traffic the Companies did not reach this point til 00.45 hours.

They were formed up as follows:-

Front line.  C. COY on right
    do       D.  "  "  left.
Support  "   A.  "  "  right.
   "     "   B.  "  "  left.

The role of the companies was as follows :-
Front line Companies to attack final objective, taking the BEAURIVOIR LINE en route

A Company to mop up and establish itself in the BEAURIVOIR LINE B Company to form the defensive flank. Battalion H.Q. established at M.35.8.3. .

At 07.00 hours, the Barrage opened.

The enemy Artillery retaliation was small and the advance to the line of BEAURIVOIR TRENCHES was carried out successfully and many Prisoners captured.

"A" Coy was held up by the wire and suffered some casualties by shell fire, the other Coys found good gaps.

The advance from the tranches up the slope to the final objective was opposed by a number of machine guns clearly sighted in the open. This resistance was overcome and the final objective was reached, the protective flank was also established.

Enemy machine guns at ARDYSSART FARM and ANGLE CHATEAU caused some casualties.

At 05.00 hours the 6th BN THE LEICESTERSHIRE REGT forming up under cover of the defensive flank advanced to attack the line HAUT FARM-HURTEBISE FARM (N27d.a.-N.2I.d.a. : with the 7th BN LEICESTERSHIRE REGT in support, to later form a defensive flank HURTEBISE FARM to N.I9.central.

At 08.00 the 62nd INF. BDE. passed through the front line and attacked WALINGCOURT.

APPENDIX. NO. 2.

OPERATIONS 22/23rd Oct. 1918.

Sheet.

On the afternoon of the 22nd the Battalion was Bivouaced in J.17d. . At 16.30 the Battalion moved off in column of route with increased distances to NEUVILLY and crossed the RIVER SELLE by plank bridge at K.1.c.5.9. and rested in K.1d.

At 22.00 the Battalion moved off by a reconnoitred route to the bend in the railway at K.2.A.1.1. and from there, guided by the Stars to the corner of the fence E.26.d.95.85. reaching this point at 22.45 hours.

The plan of operations was as follows:-

The 6th BTTN LEICESTERSHIRE REGT was holding the line(green) E.28d.1.2. to E.27b.5.7. The 7th BTN LEICESTERSHIRE REGT and the 1st BATTN WILTSHIRE REGT on the right were to attack two objectives.

The first being the line(dotted red) E.29b.8.8. to E.22.d.50.95. The second being the line (red) E.18d.5.5. to E.18a.8.9..

The Battalion rested at the corner of the fence until 00.30. During that time the enemy's artillery was active but no casualties occurred. A thick mist had collected and obscures all features on the ground. The stars were visable.

The Battalion moved off guided by the stars to a spot E.28.a.0.0. where it was to form up for the attack in two lines.
'C' Coy right of front line
'A' Coy left of front line.
'B' Coy right of second line,
'D' Coy left of second line.

The 7th BN LEICESTERSHIRE REGT on the left and the DURHAM LIGHT INFANTRY (64th INF. BDE.) on the right.

On the march to the above spot there was some shelling but no casualties. On arriving within 300 yards of this point the Battalion march out of the mist. The Battalion then halted, and the forming up tape was being laid out when the enemy artillery opened on the forming up line . The number of guns firing increased rapidly , until quite a heavy barrage came down on the forming up line causing considerable disorganisation of the Battalion and the process of laying the tape. A number of casualties occurred. The Battalion was eventually formed up and moved forward to the attack at 01.55 hours, the enemy barrage still continued. At 02.00 hours our barrage opened

The first objective was captured with some casualties caused by artillery fire and the advanced continued.

Some casualties occurred before reaching the village of OVILLERS caused by machine gun fire from the right flank. The village was captured and C. & A. Coys pushed on and reached the final objective. The remaining Coys and Unit on the left lost direction owing to the darkness. One message rocket was fired by 'C' Coy at 05.15 hours. It was seen by B.H.Q. at E.28c2.8. but could not be found.

At 07.10 hours the 6th BN LEICESTERSHIRE REGT passed through the red line to a further objective.

COMBE. 1st Bn. WILTSHIRE REGT.

## 1st Battalion Wiltshire Regiment

### Awards during the month of October, 1918.

**Military Cross**

    T/2/Lieut. R. EMMERSON      Durham L.I. att. 1st Wilts Regt.
    T/2/Lieut. J.C. KEMP, M.M.      Wilts Regt.

**D.C.M.**

    22250 Sergt. W.C. BUNDAY

**M.M.**

    203644 Sergt. W.H. Beavan
    39940 Sergt. J. Young
    34442 Sergt. S. COOPER
    18849 Cpl. A.V. GREENLAND
    10822 Cpl. T.S. HOSMER
    43880 L/cpl. E. O'HEA
    39911 L/cpl. F. MASTERS
    39879 Pte. J. FOY

Lt. Colonel,
COMDG. 1st Bn. WILTSHIRE REGT.

List of Officers at duty with Battalion during the month of October, 1918.

```
Lieut:Col.G.B.C.Ward.D.S.O.          Commanding Officer.
Major.T.G.Parkes.M.C.                2nd in Command.
Captain.C.H.Gaskell.M.C.             Company Commander.
    "   W.D.Rowe.                             -do-
    "   H.B.Brown.M.C.     (To Base 18/10/18)-do-
    "   H.H.Sabben.        (To 21st Division 8/10/18) -do-
    "   H.Webber.                    A/Quartermaster.
    "   H.T.Morgan.M.C.              A/Adjutant.
Lieut:  W.J.E.Ross.                  Wounded 23/10/18.
    "   R.Swayne.M.C.      (Joined Bn 15/10/18)
    "   G.Cartwright.      (    -do-   10/10/18) (Wounded 24/10/18)
2/  "   F.West-Kelsey.
    "   H.Stanway.         (To leave 24/10/18)
    "   F.Willis.          (    -do-  26/10/18)
    "   A.Cooke.           (    -do-  30/10/18)
    "   W.J.Bullock.M.M.             Transport Officer.
    "   A.E.Thompson.                Intelligence Officer.
    "   R.C.Spark.         (From leave 13/10/18)
    "   W.B.Mason.
        E.W.J.Duley.
    "   P.Mintrim.
    "   J.T.Luscombe.      (wounded 8/10/18)
    "   H.S.Aston.         (   -do-23/10/18)
    "   R.Hall.            (Killed 8/10/18)
    "   H.L.Palmer.        ( do    23/10/18)
    "   E.G.Blackmore.     ( Wounded 23/10/18)
    "   J.C.King.          ( Joined Bn 10/10/18)
    "   W.E.Lane.          (    -do-           )
    "   H.B.Cooper.        (    -do-           ) (Killed 23/10/18)
    "   E.W.Timms.         (    -do-           )
    "   W.E.Cooke.         (    -do-27/10/18   )
    "   W.M.B.Rees.        (    -do-           )
    "   R.B.Jones.         (    -do-           )
    "   B.Webster.         (    -do-           )
Lieut:&Q.Mr.J.T.Bamford.   (    -do-           )
```

CONFIDENTIAL

WAR DIARY

1st Bn. THE WILTSHIRE REGIMENT

NOVEMBER, 1918

VOLUME 3.

PAGES 14 -15

Army Form C. 2118.

# WAR DIARY of 1st Bn. WILTSHIRE REGIMENT
## INTELLIGENCE SUMMARY

*(Erase heading not required.)*

Volume 3   Page 14.

Instructions regarding War Diaries and Intelligence Summaries are contained in F.S. Regs., Part II. and the Staff Manual respectively. Title Pages will be prepared in manuscript.

| Place | Date | Hour | Summary of Events and Information | Remarks and references to Appendices |
|---|---|---|---|---|
| POIX-DU-NORD AMERVAL | Nov. 1 | | Strength Officers 29 other ranks 662 Horses 53 | 1st m |
| | 2 | 17.15 | Batt. proceeded by March Route to AMERVAL map reference 5.G.5.8. sheet Valenciennes 12 | 1st m Appendix No 1 |
| | 3 | 10.45 | Draft of 106 other ranks joined the Battalion. | 1st m Appendix No 2 |
| | 4 | 13.00 | Battalion proceeded to take up position for operations on Nov. 5th. Battalion first proceeded to concentration area near POIX-DU-NORD where tea was served. At 16.30 Battalion continued march to further concentration area East of ENGLEFONTAINE. Battalion H.Qrs. established at S.20.d.4.3. (sheet 51) | 1st m |
| Nr. ENGLE-FONTAINE | 5 | 08.00 | Battalion marched through FOREST DE MORMAL and was billetted in LA TETE NOIR. Battalion H.Qrs. established at T.23.d.3.3. (sheet 51) | 1st m |
| LA TETE NOIR | 6 | 03.30 | Battalion advanced through BERLAIMONT for attack on AULNOYE and LIMONT FOUNTAINE. Battalion crossed River Sambre by broken bridges at BERLAIMONT at 05.15 hours but were unable to go forward owing to heavy machine gun fire from AULNOYE. Battalion proceeded to outflank enemy who withdrew from AULNOYE. Battalion went forward and established a line on high ground East of AULNOYE and AYMERIES. Battalion H.Qrs. established at THE BREWERY, AULNOYE map sheet 51. U.22.c.3.3. | 1st m Appendix No 3 |
| Nr. AULNOYE | 7 | 05.30 | Battalion advanced and captured high ground overlooking LIMONT-FOUNTAINE (map ref. V.23.central Battalion H.Qrs. established at THE QUARRIES (V.19.b. sheet 51) | 1st m Appendix No 4 |
| | | 20.30 | Battalion proceeded by March Route to AULNOYE where it was billetted for the night. | 1st m |
| AULNOYE | 8 | 08.15 | Battalion proceeded by March Route to BERLAIMONT. Battalion H.Qrs. established at U.21.c.1.1. sheet 51. | 1st m |
| BERLAIMONT | 9 | | Strength Officers 34 other ranks 643 Horses 53 | 1st m |
| | 10 | 16.00 | Draft of 5 officers and 58 other ranks joined the Battalion | 1st m |
| | 11 | 11.00 | Instructions received that HOSTILITIES were to cease at 11.00, and that no intercourse was to be held with the enemy. Defensive measures to be taken Lieut.Col.G.B.Ward, D.S.O. returned from leave and assumed command of the Battalion | 1st m |
| | | 12.45 | Battalion proceeded by March Route to BEAUFORT. Battalion H.Qrs established at W.14.d.2.7. sheet 51. | 1st m Appendix No 5 |
| BEAUFORT | 12 | 08.30 | Reorganisation and training commenced Messages of congratulation received from GENERAL the HON. SIR JULIAN BYNG, K.C.B., K.C.G.M., M.V.O. Cmdg. 3rd Army LIEUT. GEN. C.D.SHUTE Cmdg. 5th Corps MAJOR. GEN. D.G.M.CAMPBELL Cmdg. 25th Division BRIG. GEN. H.CUMMINGS, D.S.O. 110th Infy. Bde. | 1st m Appendix No 6 No 7 No 8 1st m Appendices Nos 9-10 |

J.B.Ward Major

Cmdg. 1st Bn. Wiltshire Regt.

# WAR DIARY of 1st Bn. WILTSHIRE REGIMENT

## INTELLIGENCE SUMMARY

Volume 3   Page 15.

Army Form C. 2118.

| Place | Date | Hour | Summary of Events and Information | Remarks and references to Appendices |
|---|---|---|---|---|
| BEAUFORT | 14 | 12.30 | Lieut. Col. G.B.C.WARD, D.S.O. assumed command of the 110th Infy Bde. during the absence of Brig. Gen. H.CUMMINGS, D.S.O. on leave. | initial |
| | 16 | | Major T.G.PARKER, M.C., assumed command of the Battalion | initial |
| | 19 | | Strength Officers 32   other ranks 682   Horses 53 | initial |
| | 28 | | Draft of 2 officers and 40 other ranks joined the Battalion | initial |
| | 30 | | Draft of 57 other ranks joined the Battalion | initial |
| | | | Strength Officers 34   other ranks 747   Horses 55. | initial |

J. Parker
Major,
Cmdg. 1st Bn. Wiltshire Regt.

*Appendix No 1*

SECRET                                                                           Copy No. 13

## 1st Bn. THE WILTSHIRE REGIMENT

### OPERATION ORDER NO. 11.

Ref. Map. Valenciennes 12                                      2.11.18.

1. **Move**      The Battalion will be relieved to-night by the 9th Bn. The Duke of Wellington's Regt. and will proceed by March Route on relief to billets and camp at AMERVAL (Map Ref. 5.G.5.8. sheet Valenciennes 12.

2. **Route**      POIX-DU-NORD, ST. JOSEPH'S CHAPEL, VENDEGIES, OVILLERS - AMERVAL.

3. **Order of March**
   H.Q.
   D.Coy
   C.Coy
   B.Coy
   A.Coy

4. **Time**      Leading Coy. will not pass ST. JOSEPH'S CHAPEL before 17.15 hours.

5. **Transport**      Lewis gun limbers and officers rides will be at ST. JOSEPH'S CHAPEL.

6. **Guides**      Guides to conduct Coys to their billets will be at OVILLERS CHURCH at 21.00 hours

7. **Completion of relief**      Completion of relief will be notified by code word CALIST HENICS

8. **B.H.Q.**      B.H.Q. closes at POIX-DU-NORD at 17.15 hours and opens at AMERVAL on arrival.

9. **Acknowledge**

Issued by runner at 12.00 hours

Distribution                                          (Signed) H.T.MORGAN,
Copy No. 1    110th Infy Bde                     Capt and Adjt.
          2    O.C. 9th D. of W. Regt      1st Bn. Wiltshire Regt.
          3    O.O.
          4    O.C.A.Coy
          5    O.C.B.Coy
          6    O.C.C.Coy
          7    O.C.D.Coy
          8    O.C.H.Q.Coy
          9    T.O.
         10    Q.M.
         11    M.O.
         12    R.S.M.
         13    War Diary
         14    File

SECRET  *Appendix No 2.*  COPY NO. 12

## 1st Bn. WILTSHIRE REGIMENT.

### OPERATION ORDER NO 12

Ref. Map Valenciennes 12                    3.11.1918

1. **Move** — Battalion will move by March Route tomorrow, 4th inst, to take up positions for attack in accordance with special attack orders issued.

2. **Route** — AMERVAL - OVILLERS - VENDIGIES - POIX-DU-NORD - ENGLEFOUNTAINE

3. **Order of march** — H.Q.
    A.Coy
    B.Coy
    C.Coy
    D.Coy

4. **Starting point** — Cross Roads S.G.55.80.

5. **Time** — Head of column will pass starting point at 12.15. hours

6. **Transport** — 1st Line Transport will accompany the Battalion. Echelon B. will remain at POIX-DU-NORD. Echelon A will accompany the Battalion as arranged in special attack orders.

7. **Rations** — Tea will be served at concentration area D.
Rations for consumption of the 5th will be carried on the man

8. **B.H.Q.** — Battalion H.Qrs. closes at AMERVAL at 12.15 hours

9. **Acknowledge**

Issued by Runner 18.00 hours            (signed) H.T.MORGAN,
                                                  Capt and Adjt.
                                               1st Bn. Wiltshire Regiment

**Distribution**
Copy No. 1  110th Infy. Bde.
        2  C.O.
        3  O.C.A.Coy
        4  O.C.B.Coy
        5  O.C.C.Coy
        6  O.C.D.Coy.
        7  O.C.H.Q.Coy
        8  T.O.
        9  Q.M.
      10  M.O.
      11  R.S.M.
      12  War Diary
      13  File

Appendix No 3.

## Report on operations Nov. 4th to Nov. 7th, 1918

Ref: Map sheet 51 1/40,000
    "    " 51 S.W. 1/20,000

At 12.15 hours on November 4th the Battalion left AMERVAL where it had been billetted and proceeded towards ENGLEFONTAINE where it had been arranged that the Battalion should halt for the night prior to advancing through the FOREST de MORMAL. The Battalion halted S.W. of POIX-DU-NORD at 15.00 hours and after the men had had tea the Battalion proceeded through ENGLEFONTAINE and bivouaced on on the West side of the road about S.20.d.8.6.

Two schems were issued to the Brigade -

(a) If all plans succeeded the 110th Infy. Bde. were to go through the 62nd Infy. Bde. and the 64th Infy. Bde. and establish a line on the high ground West of BACHANT in U.18.a. and c. and U.24.a and c. (sheet 51 S.W.)

(b) If plans failed to materialize 110th Infy. Bde. was to pass through 62nd Infy. Bde. and establish a line East of FOREST de MORMAL in T.18.a and c. and T.23.b. and d. after which the 64th Infy. Bde. would go through and establish a line East of BERLAIMONT.

On the evening of Nov. 4th the 17th Division were held up at LOCQNIGNOL (T.5.a. sheet 51 S.W.) but were able to push forward early on Nov. 5th and the 62nd Infy. Bde. went forward through them and captured BERLAIMONT and established two companies across the RIVER SAMBRE about U.21.c.

This Battalion proceeded by March Route from its bivouac positions through the FOREST de MORMAL and arrival at the village of LE TETE NOIR (Map Ref. T.24.c. sheet 51 S.W.) where it was billetted for the night.

As the operations on the 5th Nov. were so successful further objectives were given to the 110th Infy. Bde. The objectives were as follows:-

1st objective    To establish a line on the high ground East of LIMONT-FONTAINE (V.15 and V.21 sheet 51) a distance of 5500 yards.

2nd objective    To establish a line along the MAUBERG - AVESNES ROAD from W.7.d.0.0. to W.25.d.3.0. (a distance of 4000 yards)

This operation was to have been carried out by the 6th Bn. The Leicestershire Regt. on the left and the 1st Bn. The Wiltshire Regt. on the right.

At 03.30 hours on the 6th November the Battalion left LA TETE NOIR and marched towards the forming up position which which was on the road in U.21.d. (sheet 51). On arriving at BERLAIMONT it was discovered that the enemy were holding AULNOYE in strength and that the crossings over the river were under heavy fire. All the bridges over the river had been blown up by the Germans in their retreat and it was very difficult to get troops across. By 06.30 the whole of the 1st Bn. The Wiltshire Regt. had crossed the river and established themselves under cover on the Eastern side but owing to the very heavy enemy fire it was impossible to go forward.

About 11.00 hours information was received that the 35th Division on the right had advanced as far as AULNOYE STATION. It was then decided that the Battalion should work around the right flank of AULNOYE village and outflank the enemy. This Movement was successfully carried out and when the enemy saw our intention he withdrew and we captured the village and rapidly went forward and established a line on the high ground in U.23.b. and d. (sheet 51) Bn. H.Q. were established in the Brewery U.22.c.2.3. (sheet 51).

During the night instructions were received that the attack would be resumed in the morning and at 05.30 hours on the 7th the leading Companies went forward with the high ground in V.15 and V.21 (sheet 51) as objectives. Little opposition was met until the Battalion reached the high ground in V.20 (sheet 51) where they came under heavy machine gun and Artillery Fire. A line was established along road in V.20 a. and along track running through V.20.a. and d. (sheet 51).

Bn. H.Q. was established at The Quarries in V.19.a. (sheet 51).

This line was held until 11.30 hours when the 64th Infy. Bde. went through to capture the line running along the MAUBERGE-AVESNES ROAD East to LIMONT-FOUNTAINE.

About 20.00 hours the Division was relieved by the 17th Division who went through to capture their objectives

SECRET            *Appendix No 4.*            COPY No. 42

## 1st Bn. Wiltshire Regiment

### Operation Order No. 12.

Map Ref. Sheet 51                                                      7.11.18.

1. **Move**     The Battalion will proceed by March Route to-night to billets at AULNOYE (map ref. U.21.d.) and proceed from there tomorrow to Billets at BERLAIMONT (map ref. U.20.c.)

2. **Route**     Quarries V.19.b. - track to Railway at V.24.b.9.9. - Cross roads U.24.a.9.9. - LES QUATRE BRAS - AULNOYE STATION BOUVIER - AULNOYE - FACTORY BRIDGE - BERLIAMONT

3. **Starting Point**     Battalion H.Qrs.

4. **Order of march**     Coys will march independently from present position and in following order from AULNOYE
    - B.H.Q.
    - A.Coy
    - B.Coy
    - C.Coy
    - D.Coy

5. **Time**     Head of column will pass starting point at AULNOYE at 08.15 hours tomorrow.

6. **Guides**     Guides to conduct Coys to billets will be at AULNOYE CHURCH tonight and at FACTORY BRIDGE, BERLAIMONT tomorrow.

7. **B.H.Q.**     Battalion H.Qrs. closes at present location at 20.00 hours and opens at destination on arrival.

8.     Acknowledge

Issued by Runner at 18.00 hours           (Signed) H.T.MORGAN
                                                           Capt and Adjt.
                                                   1st Bn. Wiltshire Regt.

### Distribution

Copy No. 1 110th Infy.Bde.
         2 C.O.
         3 O.C.A.Coy
         4 O.C.B.Coy
         5 O.C.C.Coy
         6 O.C.D.Coy
         7 O.C.H.Q.Coy
         8 Q.M.
         9 T.O.
       10 M.O
       11 R.S.M.
       12 War Diary
       13 File

Secret                       *Appendix No 5*                Copy No. 12.

## 1st Bn. Wiltshire Regiment
## Operation Order No. 14

Ref. Map Sheet 51                                                               10.11.18

1. **Move**      The Battalion will proceed by March Route tomorrow to billets at BEAUFORT (map ref W. 14.b.)

2. **Route**     BERLAIMONT LOCK BRIDGE - FACTORY HOUSE U.21.d.0.7. - AULNOYNE STATION STATION - POT-DE-VIN - LIMONT FOUNTAINE - BEAUFORT

3. **Starting Point**    Cross roads U.21.c.2.2.

4. **Time**     Head of column will pass starting point at 12.50 hours

5. **Order of march**    H.Q
                       A.Coy
                       B.Coy
                       C.Coy
                       D.Coy

6. **Transport**    1st Line Transport will accompany the Battalion

7. **Baggage**    All officers' valises, blankets (rolled in bundles of ten) stores, mess kits, etc., will be stacked at Q.M.Stores by 10.00 hours

8. **B.H.Q.**    Battalion H.Qrs. will close at BERLAIMONT at 12.00 and open at BEAUFORT on arrival

9. **Advanced Party**    Capt H.Webber and C.Q.M.S. of each Coy. will meet Staff Capt at Church BEAUFORT at 10.00 hours.

10. **Acknowledge**

Issued by runner at 18.00 hours            (Signed) H.T.MORGAN,
                                                 Capt and Adjt.
                                               1st Bn. Wiltshire Regt.

**Distribution.**
Copy No. 1 110th Infy. Bde.
       2 C.O.
       3 O.C.A.Coy
       4 O.C.B.Coy
       5 O.C.C.Coy
       6 O.C.D.Coy
       7 O.C.H.Q.Coy
       8 Q.M.
       9 T.O.
    10 R.S.M.
    11 M.O.
    12 War Diary
    13 File

# SPECIAL ORDER OF THE DAY

— BY —

**GENERAL HON. SIR J. H. G. BYNG, K.C.B., K.C.M.G., M.V.O.,**
COMMANDING THIRD ARMY.

11-11-18.

## To all Ranks of the Third Army.

The operations of the last three months have forced the enemy to sue for an armistice as a prelude to peace.

Your share in the consummation of this achievement is one that fills me with pride and admiration.

Since August 21st you have won eighteen decisive battles, you have driven the enemy back over sixty miles of country and you have captured 67,000 prisoners and 800 guns.

That is your record, gained by your ceaseless enterprise, your indomitable courage and your loyal support to your leaders.

Eleven Divisions in the four Corps (Guards 2nd 3rd and 62nd, 5th 37th 42nd and New Zealand, 17th 21st and 38th) have been continuously in action since the beginning of the advance and have borne the brunt of the operations. Other Divisions have joined and left, each one adding fresh lustre to its history.

To all ranks, to all Corps and formations, to all administrative and transport units, I tender my thanks. May your pride in your achievements be as great as mine is in the recollection of having commanded the Army in which you served.

J. BYNG, General,
Commanding Third Army.

Appendix No 4

110 Bde.
G.27/186.

5th Bn. Leic. Regt.
7th " " "
1st Bn. Wilts. Regt.
110th T.M. Battery.
C. Coy. 21st Bn. MGC.

Copy of telegram received from LIEUT.-GENERAL C.D.SHUTE, Commander of Vth Corps, timed 10.52 hrs., dated 11.11.18.

---

On the signature of the Armistice I wish to convey to all ranks of the Vth Corps my most sincere and cordial congratulations on their gallantry and endurance AAA No task has been too arduous for you AAA No difficulty too great for you to surmount AAA You have always been in the forefront of the advance AAA The prominent part taken by the Vth Corps in the defeat of the enemy has only been rendered possible by the gallant and unselfish manner in which every Officer, N.C.O. and Man in the Corps has played up for the common good AAA The Command of such troops has been an honour for me which I shall always remember AAA

---

Captain,
Brigade Major,
110th Infantry Brigade.

12.11.18.

W.D

Appendix No 8.

## 21st DIVISION SPECIAL ORDER.

Monday, 11th November 1918.

The work which the Division has done, whilst helping to win the great series of victories which have forced GERMANY to sue for peace, has been surpassed by no Division and equalled by few, if any, in the whole of the Allied Armies.

The record of the Division during the past eight months is absolutely unique.

Every Officer, N.C.O., and Man who has ever belonged to the 21st Division may well be proud of the fact, and especially those who fought so doggedly through the dark days of the Spring, and early Summer, and then returned to the attack with a spirit which no troops in this world could have surpassed.

Proud indeed may you be, and proud indeed am I to have the honour of commanding such a glorious Division during the greatest epoch making period in the history of the whole world.

Peace is not yet ensured and, until it is, I confidently rely on every Officer, N.C.O., and Man so training himself that, whatever the result of the peace negotiations may be, you will be prepared to live up to the magnificent reputation which you have so rightfully and worthily earned and which will cause the name of the 21st DIVISION to be remembered and honoured as long as our Empire exists.

David M Campbell
Major General,
Commanding 21st Division.

Appendix No 9.

## 110th INFANTRY BRIGADE

### SPECIAL ORDER OF THE DAY.

---- oOo ----  12th November, 1918.


Now that active operations have ceased, and everything points to an eventual Victorious Peace, the Brigadier wishes to place on record his appreciation of the work done by Officers, N.C.O's and Men while he has had the honour to command the 110th Infantry Brigade.

Since March 21st the Brigade has practically been continuously in action, till the announcement of the present Armistice. Never has the Brigade failed to hold positions in defence, when it was humanly possible to do so, or to obtain its objectives in attack.

The defence of EPEHY will remain in history as one of the finest feats of arms performed during the war.

At YPRES the Brigade fell back on to its final position with veteran precision and steadiness, and although greatly reduced in numbers it repelled in no uncertain manner the German attacks on the 27th, 28th and 29th April.

Its reputation for dogged and determined resistance was never more clearly shown than during the retreat in CHAMPAGNE, where although reduced to a skeleton it kept its line intact during those four strenuous days, until finally relieved by the French on the line of the VESLE and came out of action again attenuated in numbers but with its cohesion and morale still intact.

During the recent operations from 14th August onwards it has more than kept up its former record. It has never failed to obtain and hold its objectives, and at BEAULENCOURT, the MASNIERES - BEAUREVOIR Line, and finally the crossing of the SAMBRE at BERLAIMONT, it carried out difficult operations with a dash and gallantry which is beyond all praise.

every
It is a fine record and one that    Officer, N.C.O. and Man may well be proud of in the days to come.

The Brigadier congratulates all ranks on this short epitome of their record during the past eight months, and at the same time wishes to thank them for their gallantry, their cheery acceptance of hardships and privations, and their loyalty and bravery in carrying out his orders at all times.

Brigadier General,
Commdg. 110th Infantry Brigade.

Appendix No 10.

All Battalions.
T.M. Battery.
B.T.O.
-----------------

110th Bde.
Q.227/84.

    The Brigadier wishes to express his appreciation of the fine work of the first line transport during the recent operations.

    Despite conditions of exceptional severity and difficulty, the transport has never on a single occasion failed to deliver rations and ammunition to their Units up to time.

    This constitutes a splendid record which has only been obtained by the loyal and devoted efforts of all ranks of the transport.

Captain,
Staff Captain,
110th Infy. Bde.

12-11-1918.

## 1st Battalion Wiltshire Regiment

### Awards during the month of November, 1918.

#### MILITARY CROSS

    Lt/A/Capt  W.D.Rowe
    T/2/Lieut  F.Willis
    2/Lieut.   H.S.Aston
    T/2/Lieut  R.C.Spark

#### DISTINGUISHED CONDUCT MEDAL

    34132  C.Q.M.S.   W.Cox
    205676 Sgt.       J.Creed, M.M.
    26565  Pte.       J.T.Lawford
    12089  Sgt.       A.C.Lee

#### MILITARY MEDAL

    33105  C.S.M.   J.E.Pearce
    205693 Pte.     N.Brennan
    39895  Pte.     H.W.Collins
    39961  Sgt.     G.Ellis
    39928  L/cpl.   F.J.Randall
    205696 L/cpl.   H.Bayley
    39725  L/cpl.   J.Matthews
    39717  Sgt.     J.C.Newton
    204262 pte.     E.Curtise

north

List of Officers at duty with the Battaion during the month of
NOVEMBER
------------------

| | |
|---|---|
| Lieut. Col. G.B.C.Ward, D.S.O. | Leave to Paris 1/11/18 to 10/11/18 |
| | A/G.O.C. 110th Infy. Bde. 14/11/18 to 30/11/18 |
| Major T.G.Parkes, M.C. | |
| Capt.H.T.Morgan, M.C., Adjutant | |
| Capt.C.H.Gaskell, M.C. | Hospital 11/11/18 |
| Capt.W.D.Rowe, M.C. | Leave to Paris 11/11/18 to 20/11/18 |
| Capt.R.Swayne, M.C. | |
| Capt.F.West-Kelsey, | Leave to U.K. 15/11/18 |
| Capt.H.Webber, A/Q.M. | |
| 2/Lieut.W.J.Bullock, M.M. | Leave to U.K. 7/11/18 to 20/11/18 |
| 2/Lieut W.B.Mason | |
| 2/Lieut A.E.Thompson | Leave to U.K. 13/11/18 to 27/11/18 |
| 2/Lieut H.Stanway | From Leave 8/11/18 |
| 2/Lieut A.Cooke | From Leave 13/11/18 |
| 2/Lieut F.Willis, M.C. | From Leave 10/11/18 |
| 2/Lieut R.S.Spark, M.C. | |
| 2/Lieut G.R.Beauchamp, M.C. | Leave to U.K. 17/11/18 |
| 2/Lieut W.E.Lane | |
| 2/Lieut W.M.B.REES | |
| 2/Lieut R.S.Jones | Hospital 6/11/18 |
| 2/Lieut B.Webster | |
| 2/Lieut J.C.King, M.M. | |
| 2/Lieut E.W.J.Duley | |
| 2/Lieut P.Mintrim | |
| 2/Lieut W.E.Cooke | |
| 2/Lieut F.G.Comfort | Leave 28/11/18 |
| 2/Lieut E.W.Timms | |
| 2/Lieut P.S.Page, | Joined Bn. 9/11/18 |
| 2/Lieut F.L.Walker | do. |
| 2/Lieut L.E.Greenslade | do |
| 2/Lieut J.H.Arnold | do. |
| 2/Lieut F.P.Parker | do |
| 2/Lieut G.L.Willcocks | Joined Bn. 19/11/18 |
| 2/Lieut F.Greenfield | do. |
| 2/Lieut H.D.Deighton | Joined Bn. 26/11/18 |
| Lieut. J.T.Bamford | Hospital 17/11/18 |

CONFIDENTIAL.

WAR DIARY

OF

1st Bn Wiltshire Regiment.

FROM:- 1st December 1918.   TO:- 31st December 1918.

Army Form C. 2118.

# WAR DIARY
## or
## INTELLIGENCE SUMMARY
(Erase heading not required.)

1st Bn. Wiltshire Regiment Vol. III. Page 16.

Instructions regarding War Diaries and Intelligence Summaries are contained in F.S. Regs., Part II. and the Staff Manual respectively. Title Pages will be prepared in manuscript.

| Place | Date | Hour | Summary of Events and Information | Remarks and references to Appendices |
|---|---|---|---|---|
| BEAUFORT | 1 | | Strength Officers 34 Other ranks 747 Horses 58 Mules 4 | |
| | 3 | 1600 | His Majesty The King accompanied by H.R.H. the Prince of Wales and H.R.H. Prince Albert visited the Divisional Area. The Battalion less Transport marched to PONT-SUR-SAMBRE to see His Majesty pass. Lieut. Col. G.B.C.Ward, D.S.O. was in command of the 110th Infy. Bde. and was presented to His Majesty. | |
| | 7 | | Lieut. Col. G.B.C.Ward, D.S.O. returned to the Battalion from 110th Inf. Bde. and assumed command of the Battalion. | |
| | | | Draft of 35 other ranks joined the Battalion. | |
| | 13 | 0800 | Major A. Whittle, The Wiltshire Regiment joined the Battalion for duty. | |
| | | | 20 miners left for United Kingdom. | |
| | 14 | | Strength Officer 38 Other ranks 739 Horses 56 51 Mules 4 | Appendix No.1. |
| | 14 | 1000 | Battalion commenced move to CAVILLON area near AMIENS staging for the night of 14th at BERLIAMONT (Map reference 47.8.c. sheet Valenciennes 12 1/100,000) | |
| BERLIAMONT | 15 | 0900 | Battalion proceeded by march route through FOREST DE NORMAL to VENDIGIES (Map.Ref. F.7.d.2.9. sheet 57b.N.E.) | Appendix No.2 |
| VENDIGIES | 16 | 1000 | Battalion proceeded by march route to INCHY (Map Ref. J.21.b. Sheet 57b.) | Appendix No 3 |
| INCHY | 17 | 0600 | Battalion less Transport embussed and proceeded via CAMBRAI, BAPAUME, ALBERT and AMIENS to CLAIRY SAULCHOIX arriving at 15.00 hours. Battalion H.Q. established a' Billet No. C.22. Regtl. Transport commenced march to CLAIRY SAULCHOIX staging on successive nights at VILLERS OUTREAUX, TINCOURT, PROART, GLISSY LONGUEAU arriving at CLAIRY SAULCHOIX at 12.00 hours 21st December. | Appendix No 4 |
| CLAIRY SAULCHOIX | 17 | 1500 | Lieut E.S.C.Parsons, M.C. and draft of 115 other ranks joined the Battalion | |
| | 21 | | Lieut. Col. G.B.C.Ward, D.S.O. proceeded to England on leave. Major T.G.Parkes, M.C. assumed command of the Battalion | |
| | | | Strength Officers 39 Other ranks 838 Horses 56 51 Mules 4 | |
| | 22 | | Colour Party and escort consisting of 2/Lieut J.G.King, M.M. 2/Lieut E.W.Timms, 3684 R.Q.M.S. Warwick, 33105 C.S.M. Pearce, M.M. and 5613 Sgt. Smith, M.M. left to fetch colours from the Regtl. Depot, Devizes. | |
| | 24 | | Lieut.G.Cartwright, 2/Lieut L.W.Balch and draft of 4 other ranks joined Battalion | |
| | 25 | 1100 | Brigadier General H. Cummings, D.S.O., Cmdg. 110th Infy. Bde. visited all billets and officers messes. Major T.G. Parkes, M.C., Cmdg. the Battalion visited all men at their dinners. | |
| | 31 | 1100 | Colour Party and escort with Colours returned to the Battalion Strength Officers 41 Other ranks 821 Horses 58 51 Mules 4 | |

J.Clarke Major Cmdg
1ST BN. WILTSHIRE REGT.

List of Officers at duty with the Battalion during
the month of December

Lieut. Col. G.H.C.Ward, D.S.O.      A/G.O.C. 110th Infy. Bde from 1/12/18
                                    to 8/12/18
                                    Leave to U.K. 21/12/18
Major T.G.Parkes, M.C.
Major A.Whittle                     Joined Battalion 13/12/18
Capt. H.T.Morgan, M.C.   Adjutant
Capt. W.D.Rowe, M.C.
Capt. R.Swayne, M.C.
Capt. P.West-Kelsey, M.C.
Capt. H.Webber           A/Q.M.
Capt. C.H.Gaskell, M.C.             From Hospital 5/12/18
Lieut D.P.Hannam
Lieut D.F.Brown                     Joined Battalion 5/12/18
Lieut E.S.C.Parsons, M.C.              "        "    17/12/18
Lieut G.Cartwright                     "        "    24/12/18
2/Lieut W.J.Bullock, M.M.
2/Lieut H.Starway
2/Lieut W.B.Mason                   Leave to U.K. 22/12/18
2/Lieut A.E.Thompson                From Leave 7/12/18
2/Lieut A.Cooke
2/Lieut F.Willis, M.C.
2/Lieut R.C.Spark, M.C.
2/Lieut G.R.Beauchamp, M.C.         From Leave 14/12/18
2/Lieut W.E.Lane
2/Lieut W.M.B.Rees
2/Lieut B.Webster
2/Lieut J.G.King, M.M.
2/Lieut E.W.J.Duley                 Leave to U.K. 25/12/18
2/Lieut P.Mintrim
2/Lieut W.E.Cooke
2/Lieut F.G.Comfort                 From Leave 12/12/18
2/Lieut E.W.Tinous
2/Lieut P.S.Page
2/Lieut F.L.Walker
2/Lieut L.E.Greensdade
2/Lieut F.P.Parker
2/Lieut J.H.Arnold
2/Lieut G.L.Villcocks
2/Lieut F.Greenfield
2/Lieut H.D.Deighton, M.M.
2/Lieut R.S.Jones                   From Hospital 14/12/18
2/Lieut J.H.Adams                   Joined Battalion 5/12/18
2/Lieut L.W.Balch                   Joined Battalion 24/12/18

1ST. BN. WILTSHIRE REGT.

## 1st Battalion Wiltshire Regiment
### Awards during the month of December, 1918

**MILITARY CROSS**

T/2/Lieut/A/Capt. F. West-Kelsey

**BAR TO MILITARY CROSS**

Lt/A/Capt. W.D. Rowe, M.C.

*[signature]* Major
Cmdg.
1ST. BN. WILTSHIRE REGT.

SECRET                    Appendix No 1                COPY. NO. 11

## 1st Bn. Wiltshire Regt. Operation Order No. 15.

Ref. Map 51                                              12.12.1918

1. **Move**       The 1st Bn. Wiltshire Regt will proceed by march route on 14th
                  inst to BERLAIMONT

2. **Route**      As laid down in warning order issued on 11th inst.

3. **Starting Point**   Road junction W.14.d.3.8.

4. **Time**       Head of column will pass starting point at 10.05 hours.

5. **Order of march**     Band
                          H.Q.
                          C.Coy
                          D.Coy
                          A.Coy
                          B.Coy
                          Transport

6. **Dress**      Full marching order, S.B.Respirators will be carried. Steel
                  helmets will not be worn.

7. **Baggage, stores, etc.**  All blankets will be rolled in bundles of ten
                  tied and labelled and stacked outside shoemakers shop at 08.00
                  hours, 14th inst. All officers valises will be stacked at their
                  respective Coy. Officers' Messes by 08.00 hours from where they
                  will be collected. All stores (except officers' mess stores)
                  to be loaded will be sent to the Q.M.Stores by 08.00 hours.
                  All officers' mess stores will be collected from Coy. messes
                  at 09.00 hours.

8. **March discipline, intervals.**  Attention is called to order previously
                  issued.

9. **Rations**    The dinner ration and tea and sugar for consumption on the
                  14th inst. will be carried on the kitchens. Hot dinner will
                  be served as soon after arrival in new area as possible.

10. **Acknowledge**

                                                     H.F. Morgan
                                                     Capt and Adjt.
                                                     1st Bn. Wiltshire Regt.

**Distribution**
Copy No.  1      110th Infy. Bde.
          2      Cmdg. Officer
          3      2nd in Command
          4-7    O.C.Coys
          8      Q.M.
          9      T.O.
          10     R.S.M.
          11     War Diary
          12     File

Preliminary bussing instructions in connection with move of 21st Division to CAVILLON area. Ref. warning order issued 11th December, 1916.

-------------

1. Embussing will be carried out in accordance with the table below. All busses will be converted lorries each carrying 25 officers and men. Officers will be distributed amongst the convoy.
2. The busses will be consecutively numbered in chalk on the left side at the embussing point. Length of convoy 10 yards per bus.
3. It is estimated that the journey will take about 8 hours and there will be no long halt.

| Units | Date | Time to begin embussing | Quantity of Busses | Embussing point Head of Convoy | Line of Convoy | Route | Debussing point Head of Convoy | Line of Convoy |
|---|---|---|---|---|---|---|---|---|
| 12th I.B. 21 M.G.Bn. | 17 Dec. | 0600 hrs. | 108 | BEAUMONT-INCHY J.21.b.1.8. | BEAUMONT-INCHY J21b18 J22a23 J22b16 J23b10 | CAMBRAI - BOIS LATRAU- GOUZEAUCOURT - METZ - ROYAULCOURT - BAPAUME - ALBERT - AMIENS - PERRIERS - | Western exit of PERRIERS | PERRIERS - SAVEUSE road |

H.J. Morgan
Capt and Adjt.
1st Bn. Wiltshire Regt.

Appendix No. 2

SECRET                                                    COPY 12

1st Bn. Wiltshire Regiment       Ref. map Sheet 51
Operation Order No. 16.          Valenciennes

1. In continuation of Operation Order No. 15 the Battalion will continue to march to the CAVILLON area on the 15th and 16th inst. in accordance with attached table.

2. Administrative arrangements will be as laid down in Administrative instructions issued on the 11th inst.

3. Order for move by bus from INCHY on Dec. 17th will be issued later.

4. Billeting representatives will meet Capt. Webber at Area Commandants Office, Vendigies at 10.30 hours on the 15th inst and at the Area Commandants Office at Inchy at 09.45 hours on 16th inst.

5. Acknowledge

Issued by runner at 16.00 hours         H W Morgan
Distribution                               Capt and Adjt.
Copy No. 1    110th Infy. Bde.    1st Bn. Wiltshire Regt.
         2    Cmdg. Officer
         3    2nd in Command
     4-7    O.C. Coys
         8    Q.M.
         9    T.O.
       10    R.S.M.
       11    File
       12    War Diary

## 1st Bn. Wiltshire Regiment

| Date | Starting Point | Time | Order of March | Destination | Route | Remarks |
|------|---------------|------|----------------|-------------|-------|---------|
| Dec. 15. | Rd. Junction U.21c.5.9. Sheet 51 | 09.10 | H.Q. Band D.Coy A.Coy B.Coy C.Coy Transport | VENDIGIES | LOCQUIGNOL - cross rds 5/6th mile E. of Q. in LOCQUIGNOL - thence E. to road junction ¼ mile N.E. of last R in ENGLEFONTAINE - ENGLEFONTAINE - POIX du NORD - road junction 5/6th mile E. of last R. in NEUVILLE - thence south to VENDIGIES | ½ hour halt will be observed from 11.50 to 12.20 hours during which hot tea will be served |
| Dec. 16. | Rd Junction immediately N. of last R in RUE des HARPIES | 09.50 | H.Q. Band A.Coy B.Coy C.Coy D.Coy Transport | INCHY | OVILLERS - ARRIVAL - cross roads ¼ mile S. of AM RVAL Village - thence NEUVILLY - cross roads ¼ mile N. of Y in INCHY - INCHY | |

R.T.Morgan
Capt. and Adjt.
1st Bn. Wiltshire Regiment.

SECRET.    Appendix No 1                  Copy No. 3

## 110th Inf. Bde. Order No. 180.

Ref. VALENCIENNES )
     ST. QUENTIN  ) 1/100,000.           10th December, 1918.
     AMIENS       )

1. The Brigade Group will move to the CAVILLON Area by march route and bus in accordance with the attached table.

2. Separate administrative instructions are being issued.

3. Distances laid down in G.R.O.5585 of Nov. 16th, 1918, will be observed in all marches in connection with this move.
   Attention is directed to the Memorandum "March Discipline" forwarded reference G.27/102 dated 7th Decr. 1918.

4. Completion of moves of personnel and transport to new areas will be reported to Brigade Headquarters.

5. Brigade Headquarters will close at BEAUFORT at 10.00 hrs. Decr. 14th 1918, and open at BERLAIMONT at same hour.
   Further moves of Brigade H.Q. will be notified later.

6. ACKNOWLEDGE.

                                          Captain,
                                          a/Brigade Major,
                                          110th Infantry Brigade.

DISTRIBUTION:-

No. 1 - 6th Bn. Leic. Rgt.    No.11 - G. O. C.
    2 - 7th   "   "    "         12 - Staff Captain.
    3 - 1st Bn. Wilts.Rgt.       13 - Signals.
    4 - 110th T.M.Battery.       14 - Area Cmdt. BERLAIMONT.
    5 - No. 3 Coy. Train.        15 -   "     "   VENDEGIES.
    6 - a/B.T.O. (7th Leic.)     16 -   "     "   INCHY.
    7 - 65th Field Amb.          17/18 - War Diary.
    8 - 21st Bn. M.G.Corps.      19/20 - Office & file.
    9 - 21st Division "G".       21 - 64th Infantry Bde.
   10 - 62nd Infantry Bde.

Appendix "A".

## TABLE TO ACCOMPANY 110TH INF. BDE. ORDER No.180.

| DATE. | UNIT. | STARTING POINT. | TIME. | DESTINATION. | ROUTE. | REMARKS. |
|---|---|---|---|---|---|---|
| Decr. 14th. | 7th Leic. R. | Rd. jn. 300 yds. North of B of BEAUFORT. | 09.30 hrs. | BERLAIMONT. | LIMONT FONTAINE - Road running through second N of LIMONT FONTAINE - Level Crossing N.E. of BACHANT - thence by road running S.W. through BACHANT to AULNOYE - thence West through AULNOYE crossing River by Bridge 300 yds. North of G in LOCK. | Transport will accompany Units. |
| do. | 6th Leic. R. | -do- | 09.45. | -do- | | |
| do. | 1st Wilts.R. | -do- | 10.10. | -do- | | |
| do. | Bde.H.Q. and 110th T.M.B. | -do- | 10.25. | -do- | | |
| do. | No.3 Coy.Th. | -do- | 10.33. | -do- | | |
| do. | 65th Fd.Amb. | Bend in Rd. 1/8th mile S. of A of LIMONT FONTAINE. | 11.26. | -do- | | |
| Decr. 15th. | Brigade Group. | From BERLAIMONT to VENDEGIES. | | | | Transport to accompany Units. Detailed orders to be issued later. |
| 16th. | do. | From VENDEGIES to INCHY. | | | | |
| 17th. | Bde.Group, also 21st Bn. M.G.Corps. | From INCHY to CAVILLON Area (AILLY - FERRIERE - BOVILLES sub-area: 21st Bn. M.G.Corps to FREILLY). | | | | Move by bus. Detailed orders to be issued later. Transport including that of 21st Bn. MGC will move by Road under orders of a/BTO., staging as follows: 17/18th. VILLERS OUTREAUX. 18/19th. TINCOURT. 19/20th. PROYART. 20/21st. GLISY - LONGUEAU. |

10.12.18.

SECRET.　　　　　　　　　　　　　　Appendix No 2　Copy No. 3

## 110th Inf. Bde. Order No. 181.

Ref: VALENCIENNES　　　　　　　　　　　13th Decr. 1918.
Sh., 1/100,000.

1. Further to Brigade Order No.180 dated 10th Decr., the Brigade Group will move by march route to VENDEGIES and INCHY areas on the 15th and 16th Decr. respectively, in accordance with the attached March Tables "A" and "B".

2. Administrative Instructions have already been issued.

3. Distances on line of march will be as laid down in G.R.O.5556 of Novr. 16th, 1918.

4. Completion of moves and locations of Hd.Qrs. will be reported to Brigade Headquarters.

5. Orders for the move by bus from INCHY to CAVYELON area on the 17th Decr., will be issued later.

6. ACKNOWLEDGE.

　　　　　　　　　　　　　　　　　　　A.Sh.Ozanne
　　　　　　　　　　　　　　　　　　　Captain,
　　　　　　　　　　　　　　　　　　　Brigade Major,
Issued through Sigs. at 19.30 hrs.　　110th Infantry Brigade.

```
Copy No. 1 - 6th Bn. Leic. Rgt.
        2 - 7th   "    "    "
        3 - 1st Bn. Wilts.Rgt.
        4 - 110th T.M.Battery.
        5 - No.3 Coy. Train.
        6 - a/BTO., 7th Leic. R.
        7 - 65th Field Amb.
        8 - 21st Bn. M.G.Corps.
        9 - 21st Division "G".
       10 - 62nd Infantry Bde.
       11 - 64th    "      "
       12 - G.O.C.
       13 - Staff Captain.
       14 - Signals.
       15 - Area Commdt. BERLAIMONT.
       16 -   "     "    VENDEGIES.
       17 -   "     "    OVILLERS.
       18 -   "     "    INCHY.
    19/20 - War Diarys.
    21/22 - Office & File.
```

Appendix "A".

TABLE "A" to accompany 110th Inf. Bde. Order No. 101.

| Serial No. | Date | Unit. | Starting Point. | Time. | Destination. | Route. | Remarks. |
|---|---|---|---|---|---|---|---|
| 1. | 15th. | 6th Leic. R. | Level crossing immediately E. of I in BERLATION] | 0900. | VINDRINES. | LOCQUIGNOL - cross rls. 5/8th mile E. of Q in LOCQUIGNOL - thence E. to Rd. junction ½ mile N.E. of last E in ENGLEFONTAINE - ENGLEFONTAINE - 10PK ¼n Mori - Rd.junction 5/8th mile N.E. of last E in NEUVILLE - thence South to VENDEGIES. | (a) The usual 10 min. halt before each clock hour will be observed. |
| 2. | do. | 7th Lei s. R. | -do- | 0915. | -do- | | (b) ½ hour halt will be observed from 11.50 hrs. to 12.20 hrs. during which period men will be given hot soup or tea. |
| 3. | do. | 1st Wilts.R. | -do- | 0930. | -do- | | |
| 4. | do. | Bde.H.Q. & 110th Tr.M.B. | -do- | 0945. | OVILLERS. | | (c) Transport will accompany Units. |
| 5. | do. | 35th Fd.Amb. | -do- | 0940. | -do- | | |
| 6. | do. | No.3 Coy. Train. | March independently - to pass Starting point by 08.00 hrs. | | -do- | | |

NOTE :-
(1) Brigade Hd.Qrs. closes S RIALMONT 10.00 hrs. and opens OVILLERS same hour.

(2) Billetting representatives will meet the Staff Captain at the Town Commandant's office, VENDEGIES, at 10.30 hrs. on 15th inst.

Appendix No 3.

TABLE "B" to accompany 110th Inf. Bde. Order No. 131.

| Serial No. | Date Decr. | Unit | Starting Point | Time | Destination | Route | Remarks |
|---|---|---|---|---|---|---|---|
| 1. | 16th. | Bde.H.Q. & 110th T.M.B. | OVILLERS Ch. | 1008. | INCHY. | OVILLERS - ANEUVAL - cross roads ½ mile S. of ANEUVAL village - thence NEUVILLY - cross roads ¼ mile N. or Y in INCHY. -- INCHY. | (a) Usual 10 min. halts will be observed. (b) Transport will accompany Units. |
| 2. | do. | 1st Wilts.R. | Cross roads ¼ mile S. of VENDEGIES CHAU. | 1000. | -do- | | |
| 3. | do. | 7th Leic. R. | -do- | 1015. | -do- | | |
| 4. | do. | 6th Leic. R. | -do- | 1030. | -do- | | |
| 5. | do. | 65th Fd.Amb. | OVILLERS Ch. | 0945. | -do- | | |
| 6. | do. | No. 3 Coy. Train. | March independently to pass OVILLERS Ch. by 0900 hrs. | | -do- | | |

NOTE :- (1) Brigade Hd.Qrs. closes OVILLERS 11.00 hrs. and opens INCHY same hour.

(2) Billeting representatives will meet the Staff Captain at the Area Commandant's Office, INCHY, at 09.45 hrs. on 16th inst.

S E C R E T.    Appendix No 4    Copy No. 3

## 110th Inf. Bde. Order No. 482.

Reference:-
1/40,000 Sheet 57.b.
    (VALENCIENNES.            14th Decr. 1918.
1/100,000 Sheets (LENS.
    (AMIENS.

1. The 110th Inf. Bde. Group (less No. 3 Coy. Train) plus 21st Bn. M.G.Corps, will proceed by bus from INCHY to CAVILLON area on Decr. 17th, 1918, in accordance with the attached table.

2. All Busses will be consecutively numbered in chalk on the left hand side, from front to rear.
   Units will distribute their officers among their respective busses.
   Each bus will carry 25 officers and O.R.
   Road space per bus is 10 yards. Units will therefore be able to estimate their respective forming up positions in the convoy prior to embussing.
   To avoid overlapping, Units will send representatives at least a quarter of an hour before the embussing hour, to locate their respective busses.
   It is estimated that the journey will take about 8 hours.

3. Administrative Instructions and locations of Units in CAVILLON Area have been issued separately.

4. Completion of move and location of Hd.Qrs. will be reported to Brigade Hd.Qrs.

5. Brigade Hd.Qrs. closes INCHY 0800 hrs. and opens BOVELLES at a time to be notified later.

6. ACKNOWLEDGE.

                                Captain,
                          Brigade Major,
                      110th Infantry Brigade.

Issued through Sigs. 19.30 hrs.:-

Copy No. 1 - 6th Bn. Leic. Rgt.   Copy No.10 - 62nd Infantry Bde.
       2 - 7th  "   "              11 - 64th  "   "
       3 - 1st Bn. Wilts.Rgt.      12 - Area Commdt. INCHY.
       4 - 110th T.M.Battery.      13 - O.C. Convoy.
       5 - No. 3 Coy. Train.       14 - GO.C.
       6 - a/BTO. (7th Leic.R.)    15 - Staff Captain.
       7 - 85th Field Amb.         16 - Signals.
       8 - 21st Bn. M.G.Corps.     17/18 - War Diary.
       9 - 21st Division "G".      19/20 - Office & File.

Appendix "A"

TABLE accompanying 110th Inf. Bde. Order No. 132.

| Unit. | Date. | Time to commence embussing. | Nos. of busses. | Embussing point. Head of convoy. | Line of convoy. | Route. | Debussing point. Destination. |
|---|---|---|---|---|---|---|---|
| Bde.H.Q. plus 110th T.M.Bty. | Dec.17th | 0600 hrs. | Nos.1 - 5 | BEAUMONT - INCHY Rd. J.21.b.1.8. | BEAUMONT - INCHY J.21.b.1.8. J.22.a.2.3. J.22.a.2.3. J.22.b.1.6. J.22.b.1.0. | CAMBRAI - BOIS LATEAU-GOUZEAUCOURT METZ - RUYAULCOURT - BAPAUME - ALBERT - AMIENS - SALOUEL - CLAIRY - PISSY - BOVELLES. | BOVELLES Chau.Rd. Head of convoy opposite Chau. gates. BOVELLES. |
| 6th Leic.Rgt. | do. | do. | Nos.6 - 30 | -do- | -do- | -do- | CLAIRY-SALOUEL Rd. Head of convoy Rd.jctn. ½ mile N. of I in CLAIRY. GUIGNEMICOURT |
| 1st Wilts.Rgt. | do. | do. | Nos.31-57 | -do- | -do- | -do- | -do- CLAIRY Saulchoix. |
| 7th Leic.Rgt. | do. | do. | Nos.58-83 | -do- | -do- | Ditto as far as AMIENS thence SAVEUSE - FERRIERE | FERRIERE-SAVEUSE Rd. Head of convoy W.exit of FERRIERE Village FERRIERE. |
| 65th Fd.Amb. | do. | do. | Nos.84-87 | -do- | -do- | -do- | SAVEUSE - AMIENS Rd. Head of convoy SAVEUSE Ch. SAVEUSE. |
| 21st Br.MGC. | do. | do. | Nos.88-108 | -do- | -do- | Ditto as far as AMIENS thence DREUIL - BREILLY. | BREILLY - DREUIL Rd. Head of convoy Rd.jctn. W. exit of Village. BREILLY. |

P.T.O.

Appendix "L"

- 2 -

NOTE :-

(1) For information of those who do not possess 1/40,000, 57.b. map :-

Embussing Point (Head of column:- Rd. junction immediately S. of T in STA.
(Line of Convoy:- Rd. junction immediately S. of T in STA. - Rd. junction 3/8th mile
( East - thence N.E. to crossroads ¼ mile N.W. of Church - thence S. to
( main INCHY - LE CATEAU Road.

(2) 6th Leic. Rgt., after debussing, will march to GUIGNEMICOURT by road running due N. from head of convoy.

-----o 0 o-----

Appendix "A"

MOVEMENT BY BUS to area of 118th Inf. Bde. Order No. 112.

| Unit. | Date. | Time to commence embussing. | Nos. of buses. | Embussing point. Head of convoy. | Embussing point. Line of convoy. | Route. | Debussing point. | Destination. |
|---|---|---|---|---|---|---|---|---|
| E.H.Q. plus 10th T.M.B. | Dec.17th | 0600 hrs. | 1 – 6 | BEAUMONT – INCHY Rd. J.21.b.1.8. | BEAUMONT – INCHY Rd. J.21.b.1.8. J.22.a.9.3. J.22.a.6.1. J.22.b.1.6. J.22.b.1.9. | CAMBRAI – BOIS LATEAU BOTTLES Chau. Rd. – GOUZEAUCOURT – METZ – RUYAULCOURT – BAPAUME – ALBERT – AMIENS – POULENS – FERRIERES. | BOTTLES Chau. Rd. Head of convoy opposite Chau. gates. | BOUZINCOURT |
| 6 Leic.Rgt. | do. | do. | 7 – 23 | –do– | –do– | –do– | FERRIERES. SAUVEZ Rd. –Head of convoy ½ mil. of FERRIERES Village. | GUIGNEMICOURT |
| 7th Leic.Rgt. | do. | do. | 24 – 61 | –do– | –do– | –do– | –do– | FERRIERES. |
| 6th Fd. Amb. | do. | do. | 62 – 65 | –do– | –do– | –do– | SAUVEZ – AMIENS Rd. Head of convoy SAUVEZ Church. | SAUVEZ. |
| 2nd Bn.MGC. | do. | do. | 66 – 87 | –do– | –do– | Ditto as far as AMIENS thence BREUIL – BREILLY. | BREILLY – BREUIL Rd. Head of convoy Rd. jctn. E. exit of village. | BREILLY. |
| 1st Wilts.Rgt. | do. | do. | 88 – 116 | –do– | –do– | Ditto as far as AMIENS thence SALOUEL – OUELY – SAULCHOY. | ST.VVILLERS. SALOUEL Rd. Head of convoy at cross Rds. ½ mile E. of SAULCHOY. | CLAIRY SAULCHOY. |

NOTE:- (1) For information of those who do not possess 1/40,000, 57.b.map:-
(Head of column:- Rd. junction immediately S. of T in STA.
Embussing (Line of convoy:- Rd.jctn. immediately S. of T in STA. – Rd.jctn. 5/8th mile East – thence N.E. to
point. (crossroads ½ mile N.E. of Church – thence S. to main INCHY – LE QUESNE Road.

(2) 5th Leic. Rgt. aft r debussing will march to GUIGNEMICOURT.

SECRET

Appendix No 4

COPY NO. 12

## 1st Bn. Wiltshire Regiment Operation Order No. 17.

Ref. Map Valenciennes 1:  
    Adiens 1:?                                    16/12/18

1. The 1st Battalion Wilts Regt. less Transport will proceed by bus from INCHY to CAVILLON area on December 17th.

2. Busses are allotted to Coys as per attached table. All busses will be consecutively numbered from front to rear on the left hand side in chalk. Each bus will carry 26 (inclusive of officer or C.S.M. in front)

3. 2/Lieut H.Stanway and one N.C.O. per Coy will be at the embussing point at 06.40 hours to locate position of busses and inform Coy. Cmdr.

4. Coy Cmdrs will report to the Adjutant on Bus X when all their Coy have embussed. Other ranks will not be allowed to leave the bus without permission of the officer in charge. Coy. Cmdrs. and Coy. H.Q. will ride on the busses marked X on attached table.

5. Coys will proceed to embussing point in following order at will pass starting point INCHY CHURCH at a time to be notified later:-
       H.Q.
       A.Coy
       B.Coy
       C.Coy
       D.Coy
   On arrival at embussing point Coys will at once embus independently. Jerkins and great coats will be worn by all other ranks. Each man will carry his two blankets.

6. In the event of a halt during the journey the following bugle calls will be in force.
       One G. - debus
       Two G's - embus
   For final debus the Regimental call and one G. will be sounded.

7. Parties of 26 (inclusive of officer) for each bus will be told off today and will proceed to embussing point as told off for busses.

8. O.C.Coys will arrange that the busses used by their Coys are searched after final debussing to ensure that no equipment or other articles are left behind.

9. Acknowledge

                                  J H T Morgan
                                  Capt and Adjt,
                                 1st Bn. Wiltshire Regt.

Distribution
| Copy No. 1 | 110th Infy. Bde. |
| 2 | Cmdg. Officer |
| 3 | 2nd in Command |
| 4-8 | O.C.Coys |
| 9 | Q.M. |
| 10 | R.S.M. |
| 11 | File |
| 12 | War diary |

| Number of bus. | Coy. | Head of Column | Debussing Point | Destination |
|---|---|---|---|---|
| 88.x. )<br>89 )<br>90 )<br>91 )<br>92 ) | H.C. | No. 88 Bus will be opposite where VIEELY road joins CAMBRAI-LECATEAU Rd. | CLAIRY SALQUEL ROAD Head of column road junction ½ mile N. of 1 in CLAIRY | CLAIRY SAULCHOIX |
| 93.x. )<br>94 )<br>95 )<br>96 )<br>97 )<br>98 ) | A.Coy | Bus No. 93 will be opposite billet No. 13 (approx) | do. | do. |
| 99.x. )<br>100 )<br>101 )<br>102 )<br>103 )<br>104 ) | B.Coy | No. 99 Bus will be opposite billet No. 16 (approx) | do. | do. |
| 105.x. )<br>106 )<br>107 )<br>108 )<br>109 ) | C.Coy | No. 105 Bus will be opposite billet No. 8 (approx) | do. | do. |
| 110.x. )<br>111 )<br>112 )<br>113 )<br>114 )<br>115 ) | D.Coy | No. 110 Bus will be opposite billet No. 3 (approx) | do. | do. |
| 116 ) | B.H.Q. Store Bus. | | | |

x. Company H.Q.

H.Q. A. and B. Companies will cross light railway which runs across main street.

Army Form C. 2118.

# WAR DIARY Wiltshire Regt.

(Erase heading not required.) 1st Bn. Wiltshire Regt. Vol. III page 17

| Place | Date | Hour | Summary of Events and Information | Remarks and references to Appendices |
|---|---|---|---|---|
| CLAIRY | 1 | | Strength: Officers 41 Other Ranks 823 Horses: 48 Mules: 7 | |
| SAULCHOIX | 2 | | No. 33105 C.S.M. J.E. Pearce M.M. awarded D.C.M. vide Third Army Routine Order No. 1324. | |
| | | | Reinforcements 15 Other Ranks. | |
| | 4 | | Strength : Officers 41 Other Ranks 838 Horses 48 Mules 7 | |
| | 5 | | Lt. Col. G.B.C. Ward. D.S.O. rejoined from leave (U.K.) | |
| | 8 | | Reinforcements 4 Other Ranks. | |
| | 9 | | Capt. W.D.Rowe. M.C. proceeded to Senior Officers Course, Aldershot. | |
| | 11 | | Strength: Officers 40 Other Ranks 832 Horses 48 Mules 7 | |
| | 13 | | Reinforcements 7 Other Ranks. | |
| | 14 | | 2/Lt. H.D.Deighton proceeded to join 1/5 Bn. S. Staffs. Regt. | |
| | 17 | | Capt. F. West-Kelsey To U.K. for Demobilization. | |
| | 19 | | Strength: Officers 38 Other Ranks 754 Horses 48 Mules 7 | |
| | 20 | | Major T.G.Parkes. M.C. to U.K. leave. | |
| | 23 | | 2/Lt. P.S.Page to U.K. for Demobilization. | |
| | | | 2/Lt. G.R.Beauchamp M.C. To U.K. for Demobilization. | |
| | 25 | | Strength: Officers 36 Other Ranks 641 Horses 48 Mules 7 | |

Lt. COLONEL,
Commdg. 1st Bn. WILTSHIRE REGT.

Army Form C. 2118.

# WAR DIARY
## or
## INTELLIGENCE SUMMARY.

*(Erase heading not required.)* 1st Bn. Wiltshire Regt. Vol. III page 18.

| Place | Date | Hour | Summary of Events and Information | Remarks and references to Appendices |
|---|---|---|---|---|
| | 29 | | Reinforcements 3 Other Ranks. | Nil. |
| | 31 | | Reinforcements 6 Other Ranks. | Nil. |
| | | | Strength: Officers 36 Other Ranks 547 Horses 48 Mules 7 | Nil. |
| | | | Total number proceeded to U.K. for Demobilization during the month: 3 Officers 293 O/Rs | Nil. |

Lt. COLONEL.
COMDG. 1st Bn. WILTSHIRE REGT.

CONFIDENTIAL

WAR        DIARY

1st BN. WILTSHIRE REGIMENT

FEBRUARY, 1919

VOLUME 111
pages 19.

Army Form C. 2118.

# WAR DIARY

## of ~~INTELLIGENCE SUMMARY~~ 1st Bn. Wiltshire Regt. Vol. 111 page 19.

*(Erase heading not required.)*

Instructions regarding War Diaries and Intelligence Summaries are contained in F. S. Regs., Part II. and the Staff Manual respectively. Title pages will be prepared in manuscript.

| Place | Date | Hour | Summary of Events and Information | Remarks and references to Appendices |
|---|---|---|---|---|
| CLAIRY-SAULCHOIX | Feb. 1 | | Strength Officers 36 Other ranks 534 Horses 51 Mules 4 | |
| | 3 | | 30 other ranks left for Corps Concentration Camp for demobilization | |
| | 6 | | 6 other ranks left for Corps Concentration Camp for demobilization | |
| | 7 | | Capt. C.H.Gaskell, M.C. and 9 other ranks left for Corps Concentration Camp for demobilization | |
| | 8 | | Major T.G. Parkes, M.C. returned from leave to U.K. Strength officers 35 other ranks 498 horses 47 Mules 4. 2/Lieut W.E.Cooke and 22 other ranks left for Corps Concentration Camp for demobilization. | |
| | 10 | | Lieut. Col. G.B.C.Ward, D.S.O. assumed command of the 110th Infy Bde. Major T.G.Parkes, M.C. assumed command of the Battalion. 2/Lieut R.S.Jones and 6 other ranks left for Corps Concentration Camp for demobilization. | |
| | 13 | | 2/Lieut W.J.Bullock, M.M. and 9 other ranks left for Corps Concentration Camp for demobilization | |
| | 14 | | 12 other ranks left for Corps Concentration for demobilization | |
| | 15 | | Strength Officers 30 other ranks 436 Horses 37 Mules 4 | |
| | 20 | | 24 other ranks left for Corps Concentration Camp for demobilization | |
| | 22 | | Strength Officers 30 Other ranks 435 Horses 33 Mules 4 | |
| | 27 | | 15 other ranks left for Corps Concentration Camp for demobilization. Lieut. E.S.C.Parsons, M.C. 2/Lieut W.M.R.Rees, 2/Lieut B.Webster and 198 other ranks left to join 2/5th Gloucestershire Regiment to form part of the Army of Occupation. | App. 1 |
| | 28 | | Strength Officers 27 Other ranks 221 Horses 33 Mules 4. | |

T.G.Parker
Major
Cmdg. 1st Bn. Wiltshire Regt.

SECRET             Appendix No. 1             COPY NO. 5.

1st Bn. Wiltshire Regiment
Operation Order No. 17.
----------------

Clairy-Saulchoix                                                          26.2.19

1. A draft of 3 officers (Lieut. E.S.C.Parsons, M.C., (in command) 2/Lieut W.M.B.Rees and 2/Lieut B.Webster) and all available other ranks eligible and volunteering for the Army of Occupation will proceed to join the 2/5th Btn. Gloucestershire Regiment., 61st Division, tomorrow, 27th inst.

2. The party will proceed by march route to 21st Div. Reception Camp, Ailly-sur-Somme from where it will entrain to Rouen to join 61st Division.

3. The party will parade by Coys at 12.15 hours in the hutment Camp field in full marching order less packs and steel helmets which will be fixed to the packs. O.C.Coys will ensure that all water bottles are filled.

4. All blankets will be rolled in bundles of ten, securely tied and stacked by 08.30 hours at the Batt. Guard Room to be taken by lorry to Ailly-sur-Somme. O.C.A.Coy will detail 1 L'cpl and four men who are to proceed with the draft to proceed with this lorry and to act as guard. All officers valises will be at the Guard Room at 09.15 hours. All packs will be stacked at the Guard Room at 10.30 hours.

5. Rations for comsumption on 28th inst. and March 1st and 2nd will be drawn at Railhead, Ailly-sur-Somme at 11.00 hours, 27th inst. O.C.C.Coy will detail Cpl. Hall to report to Bde. Supply Officer at 11.00 hours to take over the rations from Bde. Supply Officer The unexpired portion of days rations for the 27th inst. will be sent by the Q.M. over to Reception Camp on lorry conveying blankets.
Dinners will be at 11.30 hours tomorrow.

6. Lieut. D.P.Hammam and 2/Lieut R.C.Spark, M.C. will proceed to Ailly-sur-Somme on lorry conveying blankets to make all arrangements at Div. Reception Camp for arrival of draft.

7. Acknowledge.

                                                           (Signed) H.T.MORGAN
                                                                Capt and Adjt.
Distribution                                      1st Bn. Wiltshire Regiment

     Copy No. 1.    O.C.A.Coy
                 2.    O.C.C.Coy
                 3.    Lieut E.S.C.Parsons, M.C.
                 4.    Q.M.
                 5.    War Diary
                 6.    File

CONFIDENTIAL

WAR            DIARY

1st BN. WILTSHIRE REGT.

FOR THE MONTH OF MARCH, 1919.

VOLUME 111
Page 20

Army Form C. 2118.

WAR DIARY
or
INTELLIGENCE SUMMARY.

1st Bn. Wiltshire Regt. Vol. III page 20

Instructions regarding War Diaries and Intelligence Summaries are contained in F. S. Regs., Part II. and the Staff Manual respectively. Title pages will be prepared in manuscript.

(Erase heading not required.)

| Place | Date | Hour | Summary of Events and Information | Remarks and references to Appendices |
|---|---|---|---|---|
| CLAIRY-SAULCHOIX | Mar. 1. | | Strength Officers 27 other ranks 221 horses 33 mules 4 | App. 1. |
| | 8 | | The Battalion proceed my march route to BOVELLES. Lieut. R.H.Gillett (R. Sussex Regt) rejoined Battalion. 9 other ranks proceeded to Corps Concentration Camp for demobilization | |
| | 12 | | 33 other ranks proceeded to Corps Concentration Camp for demobilization | |
| | 14 | | 2/Lieut F.P.Parker demobilized whilst on leave | |
| | 15 | | Strength Officers 27 other ranks 171 horses 9 mules Nil | |
| | 18 | | Capt. E.E.C.Iliffe, C.F. proceeded to 47th Labour Group. Capt. J.H.Cochran, M.R.C. proceeded to Base on route for U.S.A. | |
| | 20 | | 11 other ranks proceeded to Corps Concentration Camp for Demobilization. 11 other ranks proceeded to join 2/5th Bn. Gloucestershire Regt. (Army of Occupation) | |
| | 23 | | Strength Officers 27 other ranks 149 horses 7 mules Nil | |
| | 24 | | Lieut D.P.Hannam proceeded to Berkhampstead on a Course of instruction | |
| | 27 | | Capt. H.T.Morgan, M.C. (5th Bn. Welsh Regt.) 2/Lieut F.Willis (2nd Bn. D.L.I.) 2/Lieut W.E.Lane and 13 other ranks proceeded to Corps Concentration Camp for demobilization. 3 other ranks proceeded to 2/5th Bn Gloucestershire Regt. (Army of Occupation). Capt. R.Swayne, M.C. Lieut R.H.Gillett (R.Sussex Regt.) and 2/Lieut L.E.Greenslade proceeded to D.A.D.G.R. and E. 3rd Army for duty. 2/Lieut R.C.Spark M.C. and 2/Lieut A.Cooke proceeded to join 51st Btn D.L.I. (Army of Occupation.) | |
| | 29. | | Major T.G.Parkes, M.C. proceeded to 1st Lincoln Regt. to command the Cadre establishment | |
| | 30 | | 9 other ranks proceeded to Corps Concentration Camp for demobilization | |
| | 31 | | Strength Officers 17 other ranks 119 horses 6 mules Nil. | |

Lieut. Col.
Comdg. 1st Bn. Wiltshire Regt.

SECRET                                                          COPY No. 5.

## 1st Bn. Wiltshire Regiment

## Operation Order No. 18

Clairy Saulchoix                                                7.3.1919

---

1. The 1st Bn. Wiltshire Regt. will move by march route to BOVELLES tomorrow, 8th inst.

2. Battalion will parade on road outside hutment camp ready to move off at 14.00 hours.

3. Lieut. D.P.Hannam will be in charge of the parade.
   Dress - Fighting order less steel helmets.

4. Dinners will be served at 12.00 hours.

5. A lorry will report to Q.M.Stores at 09.30 hours to convey stores. All officers valises, packs, blankets rolled in bundles of ten and surplus stores will be stacked at the old Guard Room by 09.00 hours.

6. All forms, tables and other military stores will be stacked at the old Guard Room by 10.00 hours.  O.C.Works Platoon will arrange for all huts to be nailed up before the Battalion leaves and that all latrines are filled in and that the hutment camp is left scrupulously clean.

7. The Q.M. will arrange for Billeting at BOVELLES

8. Acknowledge.

                                        (Signed) H.T.MORGAN
                                             Capt. and Adjt.
                                          1st Bn. Wiltshire Regt.

Distribution
    Copy No. 1   C.O.
         2   O.C.A.Coy
         3   Q.M.
         4.  T.O.
         5.  War Diary
         6.  File

CONFIDENTIAL

WAR DIARY

1st BATTALION WILTSHIRE REGIMENT

FOR THE MONTH OF APRIL, 1919.

VOLUME 111
page 20.

Army Form C. 2118.

# WAR DIARY
## or
## INTELLIGENCE-SUMMARY.

(Erase heading not required.)

1st Bn. Wiltshire Regiment Vol. III page 21

| Place | Date | Hour | Summary of Events and Information | Remarks and references to Appendices |
|---|---|---|---|---|
| BOVELLES | Apr. 1. | | Strength Officers 17 Other ranks 119 Horses 6 Mules Nil. | 1894. |
| | 5. | | The Battalion proceeded by march route to BOUCHON | App. 1. |
| BOUCHON | 6. | | Capt. D.F. Brown, 2/Lieut H. Stanway, and 2/Lieut L.W. Balch proceeded to Corps Concentration Camp for demobilization. 2/Lieut G.L. Willcocks proceeded to D.A.D.G.R. and E. 3rd Army for duty. | ord. |
| | 13. | | 6 O.R's proceeded to Corps Concentration Camp for demobilization. 1 O.R. proceeded to join 2/5th Bn. Gloucestershire Regiment (Army of Occupation) | wsh |
| | 15. | | Strength Officers 10 Other ranks 98 Horses Nil Mules Nil | wsh |
| | 20. | | 3 O.R. to Corps Concentration Camp for demobilization. 1 O.R. proceeded to join 2/5th Bn. Gloucestershire Regt. (Army of Occupation) | wsh |
| | 22. | | Strength Officers 10. Other ranks 92 Horses Nil Mules Nil | wsh |
| | 30. | | Strength Officers 10 Other ranks 92 Horses Nil Mules Nil | wsh |

Lt. COLONEL,
COMDG. 1st Bn. WILTSHIRE REGT.

SECRET                                                                            COPY NO. 6.

## 1st Bn. WILTSHIRE REGIMENT

### Operation Order No. 19.

BOVELLES                                                                      4th April, 1919.

1. The 1st Bn. Wiltshire Regiment will move by march route to BOUCHON tomorrow, April 5th.

2. Reveille 07.00 hours
   Breakfast 07.30 hours
   The Battalion will parade on the main road at 09.30 hours
   Dress - Full marching order less greatcoats.

3. Capt. H. Webber will be in charge of the parade.

4. The undermentioned will escort the Regimental Colours:-
       2/Lieut J.H. Adams
       Sgt. Newman
       Cpl. Bateman

5. Haversack rations will be carried and the mid-day meal served on arrival at BOUCHON.

6. Two lorries will report to the Q.M. Stores at 08.00 hours to convey stores. All officers valises, blankets rolled in bundles of ten, greatcoats rolled in bundles of five and all surplus stores will be stacked at the Q.M. Stores at 07.45 hours. Cooks gear and mess gear will be stacked at Q.M. Stores at 08.00 hours.

7. R.Q.M.S. Warwick will supervise the loading of the lorries. C.Q.M.S. Scott, Pte. Garraway and six band boys will proceed with the last lorry. C.Q.M.S. Scott will see that all latrines are filled in and that the billets are left scrupulously clean.

8. The five L.D. horses under the direction of Sgt. Feltham will proceed independently.

9. Acknowledge.

                                                     (Signed) W.B. MASON,
                                                              2/Lieut & A/Adjt.
                                                   1st Bn. Wiltshire Regiment.

Distribution
Copy No. 1. C.O.
         2. O.C.A. Coy
         3. Q.M.
         4. T.O.
         5  File
         6. War Diary.

CONFIDENTIAL.

WAR DIARY

1st Battalion Wiltshire Regiment.

For the month of May 1919.

Volume III.
Page 22.

CONFIDENTIAL.

Officer i/c No:I Sub Section
    Record Office. H.Q.
      B.T.in F.&.F.

      Herewith War Diary of the Ist Battalion Wiltshire Regiment for the month of May 1919.

      Please acknowledge receipt.

                                Lieut:Colonel,
: 5 : 1919      Commanding Ist Battalion Wiltshire Regiment.

Army Form C. 2118.

# WAR DIARY

## 1st Bn Wiltshire Regt Vol III page 22.

*(Erase heading not required.)*

Instructions regarding War Diaries and Intelligence Summaries are contained in F. S. Regs., Part II. and the Staff Manual respectively. Title pages will be prepared in manuscript.

| Place | Date | Hour | Summary of Events and Information | Remarks and references to Appendices |
|---|---|---|---|---|
| Bouchon | May 1st | | Strength Officers 10 Other ranks 92. | |
| " | 2nd | | 2/Lieut J.H.Arnold and 2/Lieut F.L.Walker to Chinese Labour Corps. | |
| " | 10th | | Strenght Officers 8 Others ranks 90  1 O/R to 2/5th Gloucestershire Regt. | |
| " | 11th | | 2/Lieut F.G.Comfort to 308 P.O.W.Coy. | |
| " | 12th | | 2 O/r's Demobilised whilst on leave 2 O/r's to Hospital. | |
| " | 13th | | Strength Officers 7 Other ranks 86. | |
| " | 15th | | 11 Other ranks to U.K.for demobilization 1 o/r to Hospital. | |
| " | 17th | | 1 o/r to 2/5th Glos Regt. 1 O/r demobilised whilst on leave. 1 o/r to Hospital. | |
| " | 21st | | Strength Officers 7 Other ranks 72. | |
| " | 23rd | | 1 o/r to 2/5th Gloucestershire Regt. Lt G Cartwright posted to 308 P.O.W.Coy. | |
| " | 24th | | 2 o/r's to U.K.for Demobilization. Cadre and Band entrained for ENGLAND( appen I). | |
| " | " | | Strength Officers 5 Other Ranks 62. | |
| HARFLUER. | 25" | | Cadre, Band arrived HARFLUER CAMP | |
| " | 28 | | | |
| HAVRE | 29. | | Cadre, Band embarked for U.K. Strength 5 Offs. 60 O/Rs [signature] | |

Commanding 1st Battalion Wiltshire Regiment.

Lieut:Colonel,

S E C R E T
          1st Battalion Wiltshire Regt.          COPY No:

       Operation order No:20.

BOUCHON.                                                    23rd May, 1919

1. The Cadre plus Band will entrain for ENGLAND tomorrow May 24th.

2. Parties as already detailed will parade as follows:-

   (a) PARTY for LONGEAU: Reveille-0600 hrs, Breakfast-0630hrs, parade 0715 hrs.
       This party will be conveyed by lorry to LONGEAU where they will be billetted for the night, and entrain at 1530 hrs for HAVRE on the 25th inst.

   (b) Party for LONGPRE WX: Reveille-0700 hrs, Breakfast-0745 hrs, parade 1115 hrs.

3. Rations for the following day (both parties) will be issued at Railhead.

4. All water bottles must be filled and the unexpired portion of the day's ration carried in the haversack

5. Dinners for the 24th will be served at Railhead.

6. The undermentioned will escort the Regimental Colours:-
      Lt. J.G. King, M.M.  2/Lieut: J.H. Adams.
      Sgt. Newman.
      " Smith.

7. Acknowledge.


Distribution.

Copy No 1   C.O.
       2   O.C.A.Coy.
       3   Q.M.
       4   File.
       5   War Diary.

                                            2/Lieut & A/Adjt,
                        1st Battalion Wiltshire Regiment.